2003 EDITION
A CELEBRATION OF
HAND-HOOKED RUGS XIII

EDITOR
WYATT R. MYERS

AUTHOR
LORI MYERS

ASSISTANT EDITOR
LISA MCMULLEN

DESIGNER
CHER N. WILLIAMS

RUG PHOTOGRAPHY
IMPACT XPOZURES

ADVERTISING MANAGER
DIANA MARCUM

CHAIRMAN
M. DAVID DETWEILER

PUBLISHER
J. RICHARD NOEL

Rug Hooking magazine is published five times a year in Jan./Feb., March/April/May, June/July/Aug., Sept./Oct., and Nov./Dec. by Stackpole, Inc., 1300 Market St., Suite 202, Lemoyne, PA 17043-1420. *A Celebration of Hand-Hooked Rugs* is published annually. Contents Copyright© 2003. All rights reserved. Reproduction in whole or part without the written consent of the publisher is prohibited. Canadian GST #R137954772.

NOTICE: *All patterns and hooked pieces presented here are Copyright© the individual designers, who are named in the corresponding captions. No hooked piece presented here may be duplicated in any form without the designer's consent.*

A PUBLICATION OF

R·U·G
HOOKING

1300 MARKET ST., SUITE 202
LEMOYNE, PA 17043-1420
(717) 234-5091
(800) 233-9055
www.rughookingonline.com
rughook@paonline.com
Printed in China

ISBN 1-881982-33-5

51695 >

EAN

9 781881 982333

TABLE OF C

MW01042732

Introduction

Welcome to the future of the *Celebration* contest!

For those of you new to the craft of rug hooking, this book is the culmination of the best hand-hooked work of the year, narrowed down from 160 rugs to just 30 by our four capable and esteemed judges (see below).

For those of you familiar with our annual book ... get ready because *Celebration* just got better.

You've probably already noticed that this year's *Celebration* annual feels a little heavier in your hands. That's because we threw in eight extra pages for a total of 80 to showcase even more award-winning hand-hooked work.

But we didn't just stop there. We used this extra page space to expand our "Honorable Mention" gallery to 20 beautiful rugs! And to represent the variety of styles in this amazing art form, we gave "Honorable Mention" nods in five new categories to rugs that are often overlooked by our traditional *Celebration* categories of original rugs and commercial rugs. The new "Honorable Mention" categories include Primitive Rugs, Oriental/Ethnic Rugs, Geometric Rugs, Floral Rugs, Original Rugs, and Animal Rugs.

We expanded our "Honorable Mention" categories this year not only to increase your viewing enjoyment, but also to more accurately represent all the beautiful rugs being created out there in different shapes, sizes, and styles. We hope this expanded book will pave the way for future *Celebration* contests in which all styles are represented. See page 34 for the gorgeous results.

And on another topic, have you ever wondered just why judges pick the rugs that end up in *Celebration*? Well now you can know. Look for our new box, "In the Judges' Words," in each section of this book to see how the judges felt about every award-winning rug. Use their insight to craft your masterpiece for next year's contest.

Of course, *Celebration* will always feature plenty of what we all love to see: Big and bold photos of florals, pictorials, tapestries, scrolls, animals, humor, primitives, you name it! If you would like to see what amazing heights the fiber art of rug hooking can achieve, this is your source.

And on a sad final note, this will be my last *Celebration* annual as editor. I sincerely will miss working with all of you on both this amazing book and *Rug Hooking* magazine, but after seeing the work in *Celebration* this year, I have no doubt that the future of this fiber art is a strong one. Look forward to many years of beautiful *Celebrations* to come!—*Wyatt R. Myers*

ON THE COVER: Judy Fresk's grandsons frolic in the sand in her rug, *Matthew and Andrew at Moose Pond*. See page 64 to learn more about Judy and her rug. Photograph by Impact Xpozures.

THE CELEBRATION ICON: Anne Reeves of Carmel, California, captured this gracious garden setting that garnishes our *Celebration* icon this year. See page 42 for a full view of Anne's lovely rug, *Joys of Spring*.

Meet the Judges

What a difference a year makes! In 2002 spring seemed to be on its way in March when the judging for *Celebration XII* took place. Not so this past March. Snow was still on the ground, and the temperatures hovered between frigid and bitter. One of the judges, Michele Micarelli, barely made it here driving through snow from Connecticut. And for the first time, we were graced with a West Coast representative, Gene Shepherd from California, who asked if he needed to bring a winter coat. Little did he know what was in store!

But the judging for *Celebration XIII* went on as planned, and our four esteemed judges spent the day happily engrossed in over 150 gorgeous rugs. A special thank you goes out to these fiber artists who braved the arctic conditions to bring you this fine display. May their choices warm your heart!

Michele Micarelli. Michele has been hooking rugs since 1991 and teaches weekly classes at her home studio in New Haven, Connecticut. She is on the board of directors for the Association of Traditional Hooking Artists Region 1, as well as the McGown Northern Teachers' Workshop. Her rugs have appeared in several editions of *Celebration*, and she was the subject of a "Teacher Feature" in *Rug Hooking*'s March/April/May 2003 issue.

The esteemed judges of Celebration XIII. *From left to right: Margo White, Michele Micarelli, Abby Vakay, and Gene Shepherd.*

Gene Shepherd. Gene hails from Anaheim, California, where he serves as a minister for the First Christian Church. He was a weaver for 30 years, but he much prefers rug hooking, which he has been doing now for seven years. His rug, *Fog*, appeared in *Celebration XII*, and he has written several articles for *Rug Hooking*, including one on his recreations of FDR's rugs for the U.S. Department of the Interior for Top Cottage in Hyde Park, New York. Gene is president of the Association of Traditional Hooking Artists' Orange Coast's Classics.

Abby Vakay. Abby's rug, *Thanksgiving at Dawn*, graced the cover of *A Celebration of Hand Hooked Rugs XII* and was the latest of four selected as finalists in the competition. Known for incorporating multimedia into her rugs, Abby teaches at the Smithsonian Institution in Washington, D.C.; the Springwater Fiber Workshop in Alexandria, Virginia (near her home); the East End Artist Alliance in Long Island, New York; and at workshops throughout the U.S. and Canada. Her work has won many awards, including the 2000 People's Choice Award at the Green Mountain Rug Exhibit in Shelburne, Vermont.

Margo White. A teacher, hooker, and designer, Margo says that rugs are her passion. Margo has been named to *Early American Life*'s "Top 200 Craftspersons" list for several years and exhibits annually in the juried American Craftsmen's Show in Wilton, Connecticut. She studies folk art and furniture, as well as antique rugs for use in developing her own ideas. Her rugs have been featured in *Country Living*, *Country Home*, *Early American Life*, as well as *Rug Hooking*. Last fall, Margo's rugs were displayed in the window of the Folk Art Museum in New York City, and she continues to sell her work through them. —*Lisa McMullen*

CELEBRATION **XIII**

Showcase of
Commercial Designs and Adaptations

Review these pages carefully, then mark and mail the ballot inserted into this book to vote for the rugs you consider the best of the best. For more information on how these rugs were selected, and how the Readers'-Choice Contest is run, see page 2.

COMMERCIAL DESIGNS

Kay Bowman
New Glasgow, Nova Scotia

As a former home economics teacher for 31 years, Kay Bowman made a smooth transition from knitting to rug hooking. She had already accumulated a supply of old skirts and woolens in anticipation of the day that she would get the chance to try her hand at the craft and was more than ready to learn when her local school board sponsored a rug hooking class for the first time. Her gentle and soft-spoken teacher, Sylvia MacDonald, inspired Kay so much during those eight weeks that the smitten pupil continued to seek her teacher's tutelage for months afterward. Kay teaches rug hooking classes in her home and has taught 120 beginners, including five of her grandchildren.

Anne of Green Gables

Kay Bowman has been a collector of *Anne of Green Gables* memorabilia for many years, so it was fitting that this avid rug hooker decided to use wool, monk's cloth, and her own talents to depict this little orphan girl from Prince Edward Island in the early 1900s.

"When I signed up for a portrait course at the Nova Scotia Rug School last year, my first thought was 'It would be wonderful to hook Anne,'" she says. "After receiving permission from the Anne Authority of Prince Edward Island, I adapted a design from two greeting cards."

Kay used the cards, along with her own knowledge of the literary character, to come up with an original illustration. As a result, color planning was easy for *Anne of Green Gables*, Kay explains, because the young girl is usually portrayed wearing a green dress and a straw hat atop her carrot red hair. The only wool she dyed was for the flesh tones.

What gave the project the "spark" it needed was wool from a fellow classmate, which worked perfectly in Anne's hat, the fence, and the edge of the book clutched within Anne's arms. With the exception of the dress and flesh tones, all of the wool used was leftovers from Kay's previous projects.

Kay's greatest challenge was capturing Anne's wistful expression but, surprisingly, that endearing facial essence "just seemed to happen," and she resisted the temptation to rehook certain areas of the face. Another challenge for Kay was maintaining the texture of her primitive technique while attaining the detail she wanted for Anne using #2 and #3 cuts of wool. Anne's hair—an assortment of rusty reds—is Kay's favorite part of the rug because of its imprecise primitive flair.

The unassuming young girl standing amidst a lush sparkling countryside in *Anne of Green Gables* mirrors the lessons Kay learned in the seven weeks it took to hook the rug: That simplicity is key and that less can be more. The rug has a place of honor on an antique easel in Kay's living room. If you look closely, you will see Anne's foster parents, Matthew and Marilla, standing in front of the house.

In the Judges' Words

"Very nice ... I especially like the way the fingers breech the border in the foreground."

"Simple, yet powerful. Just enough border here to stop the piece. Great color images without taking away from the overall scene."

"Very good adaptation! Wonderful colors and a nice face."

"It's nice the way the hand breaks the border."

Anne of Green Gables, *15½" x 20¾", #2- and 3-cut wool on monk's cloth, 2002. Adapted from greeting cards.*

CELEBRATION XIII

COMMERCIAL DESIGNS

Darlene Bryan
Columbia, Missouri

Thirteen years ago, Darlene Bryan attended the estate sale of renowned rug hooker Margaret Masters. She not only bought merchandise for her antique business but also discovered a new passion. Darlene was so impressed with the artist's beautiful rugs that she bought all of her hooking supplies, some unfinished rugs, a stack of old Rug Hooking *magazines, and proceeded to teach herself the craft. Since then, Darlene has completed 18 rugs and many smaller pieces ranging from chair pads to purses. She got an honorable mention for a hooked rug in the* Columbia Art League Show *last year, and her rug* Prize Catch *tied for third place in the* Celebration IX Readers'-Choice Contest.

Be There in a Minute

Darlene Bryan loves folksy as well as realistic rug designs, especially those that tell a story. Her rug *Be There in a Minute* is no exception. Her son, a professional wildlife photographer, had snapped the picture of this leopard during one of his trips to Africa and mailed that photo along with several others to his mother. It didn't take long for Darlene to choose her next hooking project. She loved the leopard's pose and its lazy demeanor as it lounged on a tree limb. A fiber recreation of the scene seemed the perfect housewarming gift for her son and his wife's new Montana home.

For Darlene, rug hooking is like painting a picture with wool—from deciding what colors to use to framing it with stitches on the border. She likened the color planning for this project to doing a watercolor—another creative medium that she enjoys—and dip dyed and overdyed mostly off-white new wool to attain the shaded areas. She also did some marbleizing to achieve the color of the leaves and sky.

In prior projects, Darlene was accustomed to using cording and overcasting to finish edges, but for *Be There in a Minute* she decided on a different technique. She sewed rug binding on the perimeter, hooked the outer row of stitches in reverse up close to the rug binding, and then hand-stitched the binding down. "After reading in *Rug Hooking* about this way of finishing edges, I thought it made good sense, providing a bit of protection for wear on the edges," she explains. "Time will tell."

It took eight weeks for the animal to come to life under Darlene's fingers, and she admits that her favorite part of the rug is the leopard's lazy expression in his eyes and body. To achieve the animal's essence, she relied on her son's expert photography and found it invaluable to have the picture nearby, so she could glance at it as the rug progressed.

The rug is now displayed in her son's home as a memory of his African travels ... and a testament to his mother's talent.

Be There in a Minute,
43" x 32", #5- and 6-cut wool on linen, 2002. An adaptation of a photograph.

In the Judges' Words

"Very peaceful color balance and an interesting background."

"It's so real, even without a small cut of wool! I want to reach out and pet it! I also love the vivid trees and branches."

"An absolutely beautiful use of light in this piece."

COMMERCIAL DESIGNS

Basha Quilici
Forest Knolls, California

Basha Quilici was introduced to rug hooking when, as an interior designer, she co-produced a fiber and textile show. One of her vendors was a rug maker, and when Basha asked about purchasing one of her rugs, the vendor offered to teach her how to create her own. Basha wasted no time in buying a frame, pattern, hook, and scissors. She finds that rug hooking is a natural extension of her creative and artistic life. For the past three years she has merged her passion for hooking with her expertise in interior design by designing rooms in the local "Designer Showcase" around her rugs. She is a McGown-certified instructor and the newly appointed director of the Asilomar Rug School.

Bijou

Basha Quilici had long admired the paintings of a friend and knew that these canvas subjects could be transformed into wonderful fiber art. Their collaboration and idea exchange resulted in several design concepts, including a primate named *Bijou*. "*Bijou* is the monkey who as long as he keeps his master, the leopard, feeling good about himself, then the unlikely pairing continues," Basha explains. "I chose this as the first pattern in my collection to hook because I am especially attracted to cats."

Basha did all the color planning for this unusual pairing of ape vs. cat and dyed her own wool, something that she loves to do. Years ago, she had worked in the paint department of a family company, matching colors for customers. When she was no longer employed there, she discovered that she missed mixing the paints and seeing what colors she could devise. When Basha discovered wool dyeing for hooking rugs, she enthusiastically embraced the process.

Part of Basha's design involved dressing the leopard in a plush velvet robe draped majestically around him with a turban atop his head. To meet the challenge, Basha visited museums to see how the old masters painted clothing and took notice of the folds and shadows that their brushstrokes created.

Basha is also an interior designer and mosaic artist who likes to introduce different and unrelated types of materials into her creations. As a result, she had no trepidation about incorporating non-fiber pieces into her rug and transforming it into a mixed media work. She embellished *Bijou* with ribbon, gold yarn, real gems, and pearls to heighten the majesty of the period-looking costumes in which she dressed her creatures. Basha especially enjoyed seeing the faces and expressions of the leopard and monkey come to life and learned through doing this piece that she loved hooking animals.

Bijou took about a year to hook, mainly because Basha has so many other interests in her life to keep her busy. The rug is displayed on a wall in a converted barn that Basha uses as a rug hooking studio.

In the Judges' Words

"Has a very subtle, understated mixing of different materials and fibers."

"Wonderful color and striking features in the faces."

Bijou, *26" x 36", #3- and 4-cut wool and mixed media on cotton and velvet, 2001.*
Designed by Antoinette von Grone for Hues and Views, Inc.

Birds of Sarouk

COMMERCIAL DESIGNS

Nancy Tilchin
Tampa, Florida

Nancy Tilchin was visiting Nova Scotia when she saw her first hooked rugs. She decided then and there that this was something she wanted to do. When she got home, she called a rug hooking teacher who lived nearby and made an appointment to get started. "Connie Charleson and I still laugh at the memory of me standing at her doorstep asking, 'What's a swatch?'" she recalls. "On top of being my first teacher, Connie has become one of my dearest friends." Nancy used to keep busy with such pastimes as knitting, crewel embroidery, painting, and raising orchids and horses, but her passion for rug hooking has replaced almost all of them.

Love at first sight can take on many meanings and manifestations, but that is exactly what Nancy Tilchin calls it when she first laid eyes on the pattern for *Birds of Sarouk*. She envisioned the sparkling bright reds, rich royal blues, and brilliant golds but felt she needed input with the fine details.

Nancy wasted no time in enlisting the help of her teacher, Nancy Blood, to direct her on the color plan and the dyes for the Dorr wool that she would be hooking into rug warp backing. Although Nancy wanted the birds to be the main focus of the piece, she balked at first when Nancy Blood suggested she make the birds white. Nancy was afraid that the delicate winged creatures would stand out too much, be too bold, and take attention away from other aspects of the design. "But using my teacher's color, Ice Cream, and a white-to-mauve swatch, I fingered the feathers to create a pleasing picture," Nancy remarks. "It took hooking each bird at least two times to get the right effect."

Nancy always loved fingering #2 or 3 cuts because she felt it was as close to painting a picture as one could get without picking up a brush. She was accustomed to doing the technique in the past and felt comfortable using it in this project to spruce up the birds and the other motifs in the design. Using a spot with a swatch allowed her to make the feathers stand out, but it took a lot of reverse hooking to achieve the look she wanted. Hooking the birds was both her favorite, as well as the most challenging part, of her rug.

Nancy has created more than eight rugs and numerous smaller items in the nine years she has been hooking and has given many of them away to family and friends. But her beloved *Birds of Sarouk* is a rug like few others. Nancy has kept this one to herself and has it "nesting" on her living room floor for visitors to enjoy. "I think this rug is the finest work I have ever done," she says.

In the Judges' Words

"The color plan is spectacular."

"Visually stunning! This is the best use of this particular style in that it is not all boring ... this is not your grandma's rug!"

"Very bold use of color."

Birds of Sarouk, *43" x 60", #3-cut wool on rug warp, 2002. Designed by Jane McGown Flynn.*

Bradley Primitive

COMMERCIAL DESIGNS

Martha W. Adams

Hanover, Virginia

Martha W. Adams' first introduction to rug hooking dates back more than half a century, when a childhood friend asked her if she would be interested in filling in the background on her rug. She agreed, and 55 years later, her friend still has that rug. Martha took up rug hooking again in 1995 but has gone beyond doing just the background to completing intricate designs on over 32 rugs. "I do enjoy all things relating to rug hooking," she explains, "even binding, chasing wool, dyeing it, and hooking fine-cut or wide-cut rugs." She has attended the Cedar Lakes Rug Camp for the past three years and belongs to several rug hooking groups.

artha W. Adams says she fell in love with the scrolls, flowers, and giant leaves of *Bradley Primitive* when her teacher, Edith Gerver, brought in her own version of the same design to a Richmond rug hooking class. Martha sent for the commercial pattern a year later, but she didn't know the rug came in two sizes ... and she had ordered the large one. "The rug was a challenge in itself, made harder by the fact that I ordered the wrong size," she recalls. "When it arrived in two parts, oh boy."

Undaunted, Martha didn't let the 7' x 9' dimensions scare her away. On a homemade quilting frame set up like a scroll, she worked both sides from the center on out and deliberately took on the task of making certain each scroll, leaf, and flower was interesting to look at. She sought the assistance of her rug hooking friends on the trouble spots, such as the outer borders, and had fun choosing the recycled wool and planning the colors.

Dyeing the wool for *Bradley Primitive* was one of Martha's pleasures, made easier by the fact that her husband had installed a dye kitchen in the basement of their home in 1997—complete with shelving, tables, and enough room to store her vast wool collection. She used Pendleton wool skirts for the scrolls in the center and the background and soaked, married, and overdyed brown and green skirts with the color evergreen. The large green leaves were dyed with khaki over light materials, and her spot dyes were used in the veins of the leaves. To finish it off, she used cording and then whipped the edge with a combination of green and brown wool yarn. "Dyeing was kept very simple," she says. "No unusual formulas."

This particular rug is among Martha's favorites for several reasons. One is that *Bradley Primitive* won two blue ribbons—"Best in Section" and "Best in Show"—at the 2001 Virginia State Fair. The other reason is more bittersweet. "The day I ordered it, my husband died from Lou Gehrig's disease," she says. "In his memory, I call it Roy's rug. Hooking it was a labor of love and therapy. This wonderful rug honestly was my life for 11 months."

In the Judges' Words

"A masterful use of textures."

"A wonderfully executed primitive design."

"This rug has a perfect balance of color and texture. The #8-cut is used wonderfully due to the skill of the artist."

"An effective use of primitive color and texture."

Bradley Primitive, *7' x 9', #8-cut wool on linen, 2001. Designed by the Harry M. Fraser Co.*

COMMERCIAL DESIGNS

Jon Ciemiewicz
Litchfield, New Hampshire

Jon Ciemiewicz has always enjoyed crafts, so six years ago when he noticed his wife knitting during a Christmas holiday break, he felt the need to do something creative too. Months before, he had seen a demonstration of punch hooking at the New Hampshire Craftsman's Fair and found it interesting. His wife suggested he try rug hooking. Jon purchased an apple tile kit, completed it by the end of holiday break, and was "hooked." Six years later, Jon has now completed 24 different rugs. He is primarily self-taught but has attended several rug camps and hook-ins. He has also formed a hooking group at his church and has provided instruction to several beginners. This summer, Jon will teach at the Green Mountain Rug School.

Charging Elephant

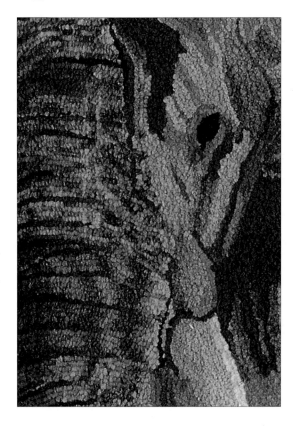

While most rug hookers turn to patterns for inspiration, Jon Ciemiewicz relies on postcards. Through postcards and his own creative mind, Jon has created numerous hand-hooked rugs depicting scenery, people, or animals throughout the years.

For *Charging Elephant*, however, Jon didn't have to look any further than his own computer screen. While surfing the Internet, he came upon artist Steve Bloom's Web site and was enthralled with the English photographer's vivid pictures of lions, leopards, and other wildlife. But it was the image of the charging elephant that really caught his eye. "As soon as I saw the picture, I knew that it was a piece I wanted to hook," says Jon. "I have liked elephants since childhood, and I immediately asked for permission to do an adaptation."

Using a printed copy of the downloaded picture, Jon drew the image by hand on polyester backing material and then searched through his wool stash for swatches that would fit his color plan. When he wasn't able to find everything he needed, he did the next best thing: He hand dyed the wool on his own using spot, dip, and casserole techniques. "I have hooked in numerous cuts but prefer to design pieces that incorporate significant detail. Using #3-cut wool provides the ability to achieve that detail," he explains. "I wanted to be able to create the illusion of cracks and ridges (for the trunk) without having to use small snippets of wool."

Other challenges awaited Jon as his work progressed on *Charging Elephant*. He was inspired by Bloom's photograph but wanted his rug to have some three-dimensional characteristics, along with the look and feel of the pachyderm's thundering movements. He was able to accomplish his goal with persistence and his usual attention to detail.

The elephant's right ear needed a considerable amount of reverse hooking to get the look he wanted. The dust cloud around the elephant's legs and trunk bottom required several episodes of hooking and reverse hooking before he was satisfied with the results. But the part of his project of which he is most proud is the tusks, as he was able to obtain the three-dimensional effect he so desired.

Charging Elephant took approximately 80 hours over a period of three months to complete, and while most of Jon's past rug creations were given away to family members, this one is proudly displayed in the hallway of his New Hampshire home.

IMAGE© STEVE BLOOM, 2003

Charging Elephant, *24" x 24", #3-cut wool on polyester, 2002. An adaptation of a photograph*

In the Judges' Words

"The color in this piece is so deep: It looks blocky at first glance and has many variations the next time you look at it. It feels like he's coming right at you, however peacefully."

"Incredible. I feel like he's running right at me!"

Judy Carter

Willow Street, Pennsylvania

Judy Carter's interest in rug hooking began with an appreciation of antique hooked rugs. The enthusiasm intensified 10 years ago when she attended a four-week rug hooking class by Pat Moyer, who taught her about color and observing the world around her. Since then, Judy has pushed aside her other projects in cross-stitch, needlepoint, crewel, embroidery, and sewing to make rug hooking her primary pursuit. "Rug hooking has become a wonderful creative outlet for me, and I look forward to many years of dyeing, designing, and hooking rugs," she says. She has completed over three dozen rug projects, and in the past four years her work has won first place and "Best in Show" at local county fairs.

Chimera

J udy Carter's greatest desire was to work on something different. As she made preparations to attend Highlands rug camp in 2002, this desire compelled her to step outside her comfort zone and try her hand at a rug design that would be a challenge from start to finish.

Chimera, with its vivid colors, lively design, and whimsical creatures, was the perfect choice. "I had seen this pattern completed in two very different color palettes and was intrigued with the variety the rug offered," she says. "After discussing the pattern and dye techniques with my teacher, I started dyeing."

Beginning the rug and balancing the colors throughout the piece turned out to be the most challenging aspects of the project for Judy. All of the wool, with the exception of the background, was hand-dyed using casserole and transitional methods. She used her teacher's technique of three colors on one piece of wool and experimented with color combinations.

Judy soon discovered that as she dyed, the colors got bolder and brighter. She found herself trying one more color to see what the results might be. When dyeing was completed, Judy became concerned that the colors were so bright that the wool would be unusable. "With careful guidance, I used all the wool I dyed and complemented them with a few extras," she says. "I continually looked at the rug from a distance and planned ahead, so the colors moved throughout the rug."

Aside from going out on a limb with color, Judy also experimented with texture in *Chimera* as well. This project was the first time in her 10 years of rug hooking that she incorporated chenille and sparkle yarn in her rug art. She found it fun to see how different textures enhanced the finished product. The animals were Judy's favorite part of the rug, as she enjoyed watching each creature develop its own personality and seeing the swirling motifs come alive.

Chimera won first place and "Best in Show" at the Lancaster County Fair and was one of the rugs that Judy presented when she applied for juried status with the Pennsylvania Guild of Craftsmen.

The rug took Judy six months to complete, and during that time, she realized she will never look at hooked rugs the same. From now on, she says, variegated textures and bright colors will be staples in her rug projects.

In the Judges' Words

"A most amazing use of color: It almost looks as if the rug is about to burst into flame."

"Outrageously beautiful saturated color. Hooray for color! Hooray!"

Chimera, *39" x 52", #4- and 6-cut wool and yarn on monk's cloth, 2002. Designed by New Earth Designs.*

COMMERCIAL DESIGNS

Mary M. Thomson
Timonium, Maryland

Mary M. Thomson put aside her Mademoiselle's Bell Pull *as soon as Donna Swanson of the Woodstock Association of Traditional Hooking Artists introduced her to designing her own rugs in 1987. That bell pull now lies in a "to do" pile while Mary designs, hooks, and wins awards for her own creations. This graphic artist used to observe her grand- mother and mother hook- ing rugs as she was growing up and calls her- self a "late bloomer" in a family of rug hookers that also includes her brother. Mary plans on hooking a collection of small round compositions to show favorite visual resources from various cultures and other media.*

The Coastal Detectives

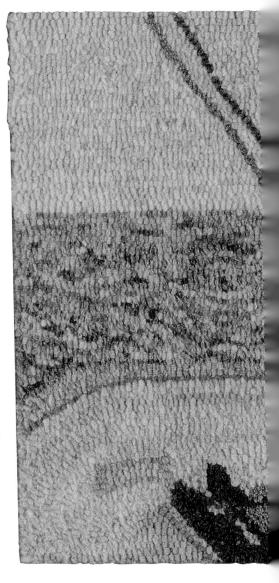

Mary M. Thomson took her workshop teacher's advice when told to "put your hook where your mouth is" after she dis- cussed with her the possibility of turning a black-and-white photograph into a hooked rug. Mary had felt for years that the photo of her husband and two friends during a deep-water fishing trip was a prime example of classic composition that spoke volumes about the friends' relationships.

As she began planning, Mary found it important to have the faces on *The Coastal Detectives* look like the charac- ters of the men in the snapshot. Her workshop teacher taught her to have a critical eye when it came to choosing fea- tures and values of colors to achieve her goal. "A day later, happiness was seeing reliable reflections of my friends' faces in the breeze of Long Island Sound," she recalls. "To round out the workshop, we agreed to limit the detail because the piece was small ... thus I went home with everything all thought out."

Mary had a difficult time finding just the right shade of blue to clothe the three hopeful fishermen. She tried some Air Force Academy blue, the darkest value, but the fabric frayed and had no light attributes. Other blue wools were neither the right color nor the right texture, but Mary continued searching. Then she read an article in *Rug Hooking* magazine entitled "Hooking with Denim" by Verna Cox, and she immediately ran to her hall closet and grabbed an old pair of jeans. They worked perfectly, and Mary was pleased that she was able to put the worn material to good use before it found its way into the trash.

Besides learning the lesson of patience as she worked on the rug, Mary also realized that sometimes a few loops of a particular color are all that's needed to accomplish your design goals. To achieve the misty, moist look she was aiming for in the background, Mary also realized the importance of clean, even textures in a rug.

The Coastal Detectives won a blue ribbon in last year's Maryland State Fair in the fine hooked pictorial category. The rug hangs above the desk in the computer room in Mary's home alongside other artwork arranged by her husband.

The Coastal Detectives,

16 ¹/₄" x 8 ³/₄", #3-cut wool on linen, 2002. An adaptation of a photograph.

In the Judges' Words

"What a vivid scene ... makes you wonder where the fish are! You can almost smell the salty air in this rug. Peaceful, yet expectant, is the theme I feel from this piece."

Barbara Jongbloed
Madison, Connecticut

Barbara Jongbloed is a Superior Court judge for the state of Connecticut. She started rug hooking five years ago after moving into an 1822 historic house with lots of floor space. With three young children, she was also looking for something to do that was both creative and productive. Her first glimpse of hand-hooked rugs made her new hobby crystal clear to her. She got a catalog, placed an order, and got the name of teacher Michele Micarelli, who offered rug hooking classes nearby. "I found hooking so relaxing and going to Michele's so much fun that I got my sister, my mother-in-law, and my best friend hooking, too," she says.

Double Scalloped Feathers

Barbara Jongbloed considered practicality, as well as style and design, when it came to choosing her second rug hooking project. She loved the colorful heirloom design of *Double Scalloped Feathers* but also desperately needed a runner to brighten up a long hallway in her older home. "Since this was only my second rug, I really had no idea what I was getting myself into," she says. "Of course, once I started hooking, I had to finish it."

Barbara began the 92" x 35" rug on her son's seventh birthday in May 1999 and completed it in October 2001. Its size was perfect for her front hallway ... but also quite daunting to Barbara as a hooking project. She needed encouragement along the way from her teacher, who did the rug's color planning and dyeing, and from her sister, who is also a rug hooker.

As a newcomer, Barbara found that the most challenging part of the rug was the scrolls. Not only were there many of them, but she found it difficult to get the correct angle of the curve and the blending of the colors. "I wanted the colors at the end of the scrolls to be coordinated, but not in a precise pattern," she says.

Barbara was also able to make this a true heirloom piece containing some personal

significance. She created the dark veining in the scrolls from an old burgundy paisley skirt her mother used to wear. Barbara's mother passed away several years ago, and the rug now has even more personal meaning.

Her favorite part of the rug turned out to be the roses in the center. Barbara took pleasure in watching them come alive as she added each new strip of red, pink, and orange wool. She finished the rug by whip stitching with a mixture of colors over cording with tape applied first.

Barbara learned to be persistent while creating this rug and has taken that lesson to heart. She has now completed three rugs and is working on her fourth, a pictorial.

In the Judges' Words

"One of the most beautifully balanced rugs in the competition."

Double Scalloped Feathers, *92" x 35", #4-, 5-, and 6-cut wool on linen, 2001. An Heirloom Pattern by Louise Hunter Zeiser.*

Jan Winter
Hollywood, California

Jan Winter thought that quiltmaking would be the hobby she would enjoy into her twilight years after trying almost every other craft there is, including macramé, needlepoint, and crochet. That was until 1992, when she attended a workshop called "Hooked on Appliqué" and decided that she wanted to try making rugs. Since then, Jan's work has won several "Best in Show" awards at county and state fairs and has been selected for past editions of A Celebration of Hand-Hooked Rugs. She is founder and former director of Cambria Pines Rug Camp and still attends as a student. She is a self-admitted "fabriholic" and contends that a rug hooker can never have too much fabric in her stash.

Flamboyancy

Jan Winter took two long years waffling over whether to hook *Flamboyancy* as her next rug project. Her first impression was that it resembled the "flower power" daisies from the 1960s. But upon another look at the big, bold motifs, she was reminded of exploding fireworks.

Jan kept the fireworks theme in mind as she did the color planning, her favorite part of any rug hooking project. She wanted to create a July 4 finale feeling and envisioned a red, blue, and purple color scheme.

But as she began hooking, she realized that some of her pre-planning would have to change. "Some of my ideas evolved as I hooked," she says. "For example, the blue flowers were going to be closer to a medium navy blue, but when I hooked them, they disappeared into the purple background. I had to re-dye the material a brighter blue."

Creating a rug that was vibrant both in color and movement was Jan's greatest challenge. To achieve the three-dimensional effect along with a sense of motion in each motif, Jan used tweeds and plaids, as well as changing color values within each "spoke." She also tried to make some of the motifs lighter on the tips and darker on the bottom to suggest a light source, and she loved the multi-layered effect she was able to achieve.

With all the different types of colors and values she likes to use, Jan finds it helpful to keep a big stash of commercial and overdyed plaids and solids for her "paints." "The bigger your wool color palette, the more interesting your rugs will be," she says.

Interesting color combinations motivate Jan, and she never thinks about where the rug will end up once it's finished. "Sometimes it's a problem when the rug doesn't really fit in with our house colors," she explains. "It's certainly true in this case, as I don't have blue and purple in my home. It may find its way into my husband's office, as he seems to like it and doesn't care if it goes with anything."

In the Judges' Words

"Bursting with movement, color, and, at next glance, texture."

"This is a very effective use of color. The artist took a relatively simple design and really made it work through use of color and fine technique."

Flamboyancy, *36" x 60", #8-cut wool on linen, 2002. Designed by Mildred Sprout.*

Roland Nunn
Orinda, California

Roland Nunn credits his rug hooking teachers for the instruction and assistance they have given him throughout his 13 years of hooking. He has completed mostly commercial kits but recently has been hooking one-of-a-kind patterns, as well as doing almost all of his own dyeing and color planning. He is a member of the McGown Guild and the former president and treasurer of the Peninsula Rugmaker's Guild in San Jose, California. Roland has contributed works to the local guild's exhibits at the Santa Clara County Fair. Over a period of several years, he has received a number of awards, include two "Best in Show" awards.

Hummingbirds

Roland Nunn caught the hooking bug from his mother, who was making rugs in the 1950s. In 1990, he made the decision to learn all he could about the fiber art his mother loved because he wanted to have a sit-down hobby for his later years. A retired chemist, Roland approached his rug projects as he would an exciting experiment or a new formula being concocted in his laboratory. To date, he has completed over 20 pieces.

The one-of-a-kind pattern for *Hummingbirds* was prepared for him by Jane Olson of the Rug Studio in Hawthorne, California, but Roland planned his own colors using Dorr natural wool in #3 cuts, which he prefers hooking to achieve realism. While most of the colors he chose for the birds were based on actual hummingbirds, he did want to add sparkle to the piece. He included some decorative thread to simulate fluorescence in the winged creatures.

Roland's scientific background and the ability to find logical solutions became useful when he ran into a problem. He had to figure out how to paintbrush dye a single piece of wool measuring 4' wide by 13' long, which he would use for the sky. "I put the huge piece of wool over a 4' x 8' piece of plywood on saw horses," he explains, "painted half the piece, painted the other half, wrapped it all in aluminum foil, and baked at 300 degrees for one hour."

To finish the piece, Roland used beads wrapped with dyed wool yarn for the edge. He then slid screen molding under the rug tape to act as an internal frame.

Roland chose this design because his daughter loved it and specifically requested he do it for her. The rug was exhibited at the 2002 conference at Asilomar Rug School and now has a permanent place of honor in his daughter's dining room.

In the Judges' Words

"Amazing detail!"

"The sky is so soft. And there are lighter values of the darker colors throughout the design, so the whole piece comes together nicely."

Hummingbirds, *36" x 48", #3-cut wool on monk's cloth, 2002. Designed by Jane Olson.*

Mammoth Flowers

CELEBRATION XIII

COMMERCIAL DESIGNS

Anne Eastwood
Venice, Florida

Anne Eastwood's motto is "have hook, will travel," and for over 50 years her rug art was never far behind. Growing up, she was taught to knit scarves, mittens, and gloves by her mother and grandmother. Then in 1952, her husband's grandmother showed her how to hook. Nine years later, Anne took lessons from a McGown teacher and became a certified teacher herself. She has taught at rug hooking camps in 12 states across the country, as well as at the Museum of American Folk Art in New York City. Her works have won first prize at the Eastern States Expo, "Best In Show" at the Lake Placid County Fair, and two of her hooked rugs hung in the lobby of the Empire State Building.

When Anne Eastwood moved into her new Florida home in 1999, she decided what was missing was a bright runner with tropical flair for her front hallway. Lack of time forced her to postpone the project, until the day she sat down to watch Jane Halliwell demonstrating hooking with 1/2"-wide strips on a television show.

Up to this time, Anne preferred a tiny #3 or 4 cut of wool. She soon realized, however, that the technique she saw on the TV screen would be perfect for a floral-patterned rug to enliven her windowless space. She asked Jeanette Szatkowski of the Harry M. Fraser Co. to design the pattern, and Anne got to work.

Anne always enjoyed devising new formulas and dyeing wool. For *Mammoth Flowers* she used six different formulas for the flowers. Then, she overdyed wool leftover from past projects and came up with a perfect antique dark brown background.

Anne dip dyed the flowers and leaves from dark to light using a combination of dip, casserole, and Laverne Brescia's scroll method before spot dyeing the leaves' veins and stems. "My bright color choices were perfect," she remarks. "My grandfather grew many colorful flowers while I was young and instilled in me the love of plants and God's beautiful creations."

The most challenging aspect of the project for Anne was continuing the light shade

26

---

*"Amazing! I've never seen a #10 cut hooked and shaded
as if it were a fine-cut rug."*

"Beautiful wide-cut shading."

---

*"Superb effect, even with such a wide cut.
The width of cut does not limit a fine artist!"*

---

along the edge of the upper petals against the dark shade of those that lie underneath. Her solution was to taper the ends of the strips to about ¼" and hide them under an adjacent loop if too many were in one area.

Anne used to think a #3 cut was the best form of hooking, and although her appreciation for fine shading has never left her, her love for wide cuts has grown. *Mammoth Flowers* was Anne's introduction to hooking with a wider cut, and she learned she could hook a large rug such as this one, which measures 96" x 36", very quickly. She is now hooking a matching flower pillow and readily admits her newfound addiction to wide cuts. "Fine shading is rewarding when I make a peach look like a peach or a cat look like a cat," she says. "It is even more exciting when one can hook wide cuts and make a good impression of an animal, house, or flower."

Mammoth Flowers,
*96" x 36", #10 (¹/₂")-cut wool
on linen, 2002. Designed by
the Harry M. Fraser Co.*

COMMERCIAL DESIGNS

Carol Scherer
Dayton, Maryland

Carol Scherer, a retired registered nurse, got involved in rug hooking 20 years ago after seeing the work of a friend who did tapestry hooking. The friend then took her to a rug show, and the work of the expert rug hookers she saw started Carol down the road to rug hooking. She has since hooked 10 rugs and numerous chair seats. Carol hooks mostly commercial patterns and loves hooking tapestries. But she has allowed her artistic bent to take over from time to time and has done original designs from greeting cards and a copyright-free stained glass design book.

November

Carol Scherer loves the outdoors and anything having to do with nature. When she saw this pattern containing resplendent fall leaves in *Rug Hooking* magazine, she knew she wanted to make it her next rug hooking project.

She asked her teacher, Nancy Blood, to come up with a color plan that would be similar to a leaf pillow that Carol had liked at a rug show. "I told her to just be inspired for the rest of it, since I have seen many of Nancy's color plans hooked and had full confidence in her ability to think in color and then replicate that vision in the dye pot," says Carol.

Carol was thrilled with the dyeing results and got to work hooking. She chose rug warp for the backing because she liked the heaviness and strength it had for supporting all the loops that had to be pulled through it.

One of the biggest challenges for Carol was balancing the color. As she started the rug, she thought that maybe the yellows, golds, and oranges were too bright and jokingly asked Nancy if they would glow in the dark. Carol was able to control the vibrancy of the bright colors by hooking the lighter values next to the background to "heat it up" and the darker values against the background to "cool it down."

Carol ended up enjoying balancing the colors so much that she says this is one rug she wouldn't mind working on again. Now she loves the way all the colors interlock and interplay with each other, much like nature itself.

Carol confronted another potential problem with the acorns in her rug. "At first they seemed 'pregnant,'" she laughs. "But after I got them hooked and the background was pulled in around them, they seemed to nestle into the piece better."

November won a first place award at the Maryland State Fair, and Carol gave the rug as a gift to her neighbor and long-time friend of 38 years, who is painting a wall in her condominium on which to hang it.

In the Judges' Words

"A nice use of dip dyes."

"A very good use of leaf colors with a nice dark background."

"Fantastic shading."

November, *36" x 58", #3-cut wool on rug warp, 2002. Designed by Jane McGown Flynn.*

Margaret (Peggy) Hannum
Lancaster, Pennsylvania

Peggy Hannum took up rug hooking 25 years ago as a diversion from the demands of her high school teaching career. Now retired from the schoolroom, Peggy teaches rug hooking to about 35 students and through them has learned a great deal about primitives. She loves using #3- and 4-cut wool and enjoys dyeing even more than she does hooking. She is a historian for the National Guild of Pearl K. McGown Rug Hookrafters and has written numerous articles for their newsletter. Her rugs were selected for three previous editions of A Celebration of Hand-Hooked Rugs and have won six awards in four years at the juried Pennsylvania Designer Craftsmen's Annual Gallery Show.

Unicorn in Captivity

Peggy Hannum actually began *Unicorn in Captivity* almost 20 years ago. She even took a trip to New York City to see the actual tapestry hanging at The Cloisters at the Metropolitan Museum of Art because she wanted to duplicate the color scheme of the original. Upon arrival, she found that The Cloisters was closed for renovations, so instead she purchased the poster from the museum gift shop.

Peggy started out by dyeing the wool for the unicorn, the fence, and the pomegranate tree and in the following years hooked the rug off and on between other projects, finishing the unicorn and half the fence. She then temporarily put aside her interest in pictorials and instead hooked other kinds of rug designs. "As it goes with hookers, our projects run far ahead of our hands, and the unicorn took a very long vacation," Peggy explains. "In the ensuing years, my husband admired each new finished project, and he would ask, 'When are you going to finish the unicorn?'"

Peggy finally took the hint last year and picked up the unicorn again. She had postponed the project for such a long time, however, that she had run out of the wool used on the fence that she dyed almost 20 years before. She still had the formula, but with the new dyes the shades were slightly brighter. To resolve the problem, Peggy wet the original piece and dipped the new swatch in a tea bath until it matched. The experience taught her to keep good notes on dye formulas in the future.

Peggy originally thought that hooking the numerous little flowers would be tedious and was prepared to just do them quickly with very little shading. Instead she found herself getting caught up in shading each one. "It was kind of relaxing to do one or two small clumps of leaves or blossoms each evening," she says. "In about four months I had it finished."

The commercial pattern for *Unicorn in Captivity* had been discontinued years before, and Peggy considers herself fortunate that she purchased it long ago. The rug was completed just in time for Peggy to present it to her husband for the couple's 50th wedding anniversary and is now displayed in their home's front hallway.

In the Judges' Words

"The colors of this piece work very well with the dark background."

"This is a complicated design for a rug hooker, but it's extremely well executed."

Unicorn in Captivity, *24" x 36", #3-cut wool on burlap, 2002. Designed by Pearl McGown.*

Joan H. Strausbaugh
Biglerville, Pennsylvania

Rug hooking has been a tradition in Joan H. Strausbaugh's family for four generations. Her grandmother used to hook with cotton T-shirts or Danskins on craft burlap and successfully sold many of her designs. Joan decided to break that tradition and use recycled wool she finds at yard sales and rummage sales. She has completed almost 50 rugs, as well as chair pads, Christmas stockings, pins, and other assorted items. She won a blue ribbon on the same rug at three different fairs, as well as winning a "Best in Show." She makes it a point to enter her work at local fairs to get more people interested in the art of rug hooking.

Whirlpool

The pattern for *Whirlpool* seemed to follow Joan H. Strausbaugh almost everywhere she went. She was intrigued by it after seeing it as a hooked rug in a book and then came upon it again in *A Celebration of Hand-Hooked Rugs V*. Then one day at her local rug hooking group, a former member brought in boxes of wool swatches and patterns. "We gathered around, cooing and laughing, pulling out pattern after pattern," Joan recalls. "There it was! The *Whirlpool*! I had to have it."

Whirlpool was the first pattern that Joan had ever purchased. Most of her previous rugs had been geometrics, and her approach to this project was to think of it as just another geometric with no straight lines. With all of the swirling shapes in the complicated design, Joan was determined to keep her color choices simple. She selected peacock blue and silver gray green and then experimented with coral but found it too close to "Mercurochrome."

Joan also played around with the blue and green color scheme by dipping, spotting, and salt shaker dyeing. At rug camp she was shown a piece of orange with just a hint of blue and green running through it and knew it would make the perfect complement to her selections.

Joan allowed each color to work its way into the design. She started in the center and let the color flow "like a spilled can of paint." What really helped her was hooking a few landmark areas on both sides of the rug and then allowing the color to work on its own out and away from those landmarks she had established.

Despite all the effort that Joan put into hooking the rug, she says her favorite part is the back. "It looks like a tile mosaic," she says. "My grandmother pointed out the importance of a pretty back by explaining that in her mother's house, the rugs were kept face down on the floor in the parlor. When the preacher came, they were turned over to show their fronts. The backs were what the family saw and thus had to be neatly done."

With a name like *Whirlpool*, this rug definitely has found an appropriate place for display. When Joan's friends finally finished a bathroom in their house that had been under construction for three years, they left the sound of a toilet flushing as a message on Joan's answering machine. She proudly presented the finished rug to them for display in this new addition to their home.

In the Judges' Words

"Looks like a very free use of color, but at the same time, you can tell it took much planning to achieve this."

"Oh, this is my favorite! Look at that movement and use of color complements with a neutral background!"

Whirlpool, *24" x 36", #6-cut wool on Scottish burlap, 2002. Designed by Pearl McGown.*

Honorable Mention Gallery

To represent the vast variety of styles and techniques employed by artists in the rug hooking world today, we are proud to bring you an "Honorable Mention Gallery" that more accurately represents this diversity. Aside from the top 30 *Celebration* rugs, each of the rugs on the next 10 pages scored the highest judges' marks in the category in which it is presented. We hope this presentation can lead to a bolder, more diverse future for the *Celebration* contest as a whole.

Primitive/Wide-Cut Rugs

This gallery honors rugs "primitive" in style or hooked with a #6-cut strip or wider.

Ballerina, *36" x 36", #8¹/2-cut wool on linen. Designed and hooked by Lamonta Pierson, Hollywood, California, 2002.*

PHOTOGRAPH COURTESY OF LAMONTA PIERSON

Family, *34" x 41", #7-cut wool on monk's cloth. Designed and hooked by Judith Ivry, New York, New York, 2002.*

PHOTOGRAPH COURTESY OF JUDITH IVRY

Master, I Am Free, *22" x 30", #6-, 7-, and 8-cut wool on monk's cloth. Designed and hooked by Molly Colegrove, Canandaigua, New York, 2002.*

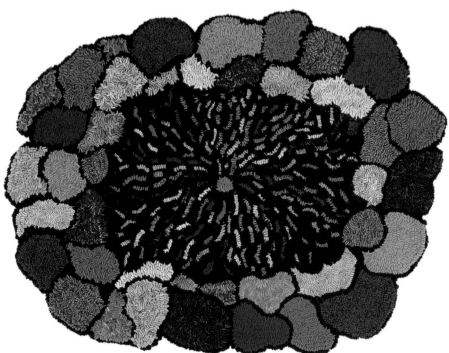

Wanderlust, *44" x 33", hand-cut wool on linen. Designed and hooked by Carrie Bell Jacobus, Oradell, New Jersey, 2002.*

Oriental/Ethnic/Geometric Rugs

This gallery honors rugs with a traditional Oriental, ethnic, or geometric patterned scheme throughout the rug.

Chinese Scroll, *64" x 42", #4-, 5-, and 6-cut wool on rug warp. Designed by Anne Ashworth. Hooked by Karen Maddox, Kerrville, Texas, 2002.*

Kermit Caravan, *72" x 43", #3- and 4-cut wool on rug warp. Designed by Jane McGown Flynn. Hooked by Edith Gerver, Washington, D.C., 2002.*

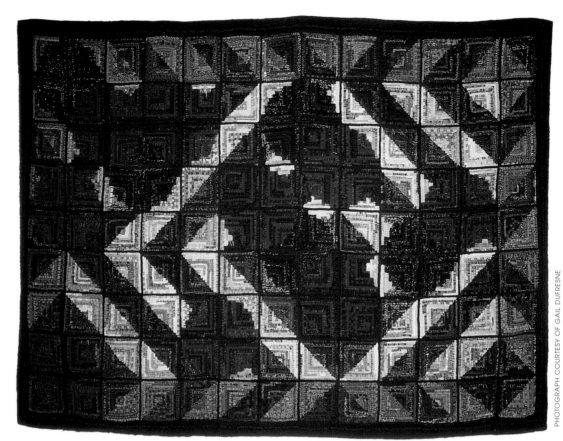

PHOTOGRAPH COURTESY OF GAIL DUFRESNE

Log Cabin Spin, *69" x 49", #8-cut wool on linen. Designed by Georgia Bonesteel.*
Hooked by Gail Dufresne, Lambertville, New Jersey, 2001.

Shanghai, *60" x 39", #3-cut wool on polyester. An adaptation of a traditional Chinese pattern.*
Hooked by Gloria Schoppe, Ardsley, Pennsylvania, 2002.

Floral Rugs

This gallery honors rugs devoted almost entirely to floral motifs.

PHOTOGRAPH COURTESY OF MERIAM BLAIR

Alliance, *43" x 28", #3- and 4-cut wool on linen. Designed by Pearl McGown. Hooked by Meriam Blair, Jefferson, Texas, 2002.*

Lilies Closeup, *34" x 28", #6-cut wool and proddy strips on linen. Designed by Jane Halliwell. Hooked by Betty Kerr, Chestertown, Maryland, 2002.*

Masterful Morris, *55" x 37", #3-cut wool on monk's cloth. Designed by Jane McGown Flynn. Hooked by Cindy Irwin, Pequea, Pennsylvania, 2002.*

My Secret Garden, *18" x 36", #3- and 6-cut wool on linen. Designed by Melody Hoops. Hooked by Ramona Maddox, Chattanooga, Tennessee, 2002.*

Originals/Adaptations

This gallery honors rugs based on an original design or adapted from a painting or a photograph.

Andrew Loves Milk, *28" x 24", #4-cut wool on linen. Designed and hooked by Debbi Gable, Elk Grove, California, 2001.*

Carnation, Lily, Lily, Rose, *36" x 36", #3-cut wool on linen. An adaptation of the painting by John Singer Sargent. Hooked by Ginny Byrne, Greenville, South Carolina, 2002.*

Joys of Spring, *22¹/2" x 14", #3-cut wool on monk's cloth. An adaptation of a photograph. Hooked by Anne Reeves, Carmel, California, 2002.*

Still Life #3 with Tea Pot, *16" x 23¹/2", #3-cut wool on linen. Designed and hooked by Carol Koerner, Bethesda, Maryland, 2002.*

Animal Rugs

*This gallery honors rugs in which an animal is the primary
focus or motif of the design.*

PHOTOGRAPH COURTESY OF THE COLLECTION OF THE STEWART HALL ART GALLERY.
MONTREAL, QUEBEC, CANADA

Global Warming Grenfell,
*31¹/2" x 19¹/2", hosiery on Scottish
burlap. Designed by Judith Dallegret.
Hooked by Judith Dallegret, Joanne
Kuntz, Lorraine Retfalvi, and Maureen
Rowe, Pointe Claire, Quebec, 2002.*

I Am A Bird, *23¹/2" x 45", #6-cut wool on linen.
Designed and hooked by Ronnie Arena, Coopersburg,
Virginia, 2002.*

COURTESY OF PAMELA W. GORDON

Peter Oliver, *14" in diameter, hand-cut wool on rug warp.*
Designed and hooked by Jennifer Parslow, Canajoharie,
New York, 2002.

Trout, *53" x 20", #4-, 5-, and 6-cut wool on Scottish burlap.*
Designed by Keith Kemmer. Hooked by Kris Miller, Howell, Michigan, 2001.

Showcase of
Original Designs

Review these pages carefully, then mark and mail the ballot inserted into this book to vote for the rugs you consider the best of the best. For more information on how these rugs were selected, and how the Readers'-Choice Contest is run, see page 2.

All These Things...

CELEBRATION XIII
ORIGINAL DESIGNS

Sarah L. Province
Silver Spring, Maryland

Sarah L. Province has no aspirations to teach rug hooking. She just enjoys it and loves sharing her work with her family. Besides keeping busy with her rug projects, Sarah is experimenting with purses made from a variety of fiber arts including yarn, appliqué, buttons, and jewelry. "My mother hooked all the rugs in our home," she says. "When I started furnishing my own home, I thought about those lovely rugs my mother had hooked." Sarah has been creating rugs for the past 30 years and has completed 10 wallhangings about her family's history. This is her seventh appearance in **A Celebration of Hand-Hooked Rugs.**

A*ll These Things* ... captures a moment in time and happy memories for Sarah L. Province. It was during an antiquing trip to Maine that the family took a boat from Boothbay Harbor to Squirrel Island where her daughters had fun playing on the beach. Sarah took a picture that to her conveyed the joy of childhood, nature's beauty, and a special family vacation. She held onto that snapshot, promising herself that she would hook it someday.

As she was getting ready to put the design onto linen, she remembered another family beach outing in New Jersey where she recalled her daughter, Susan, singing a favorite song that included the lyric, "All these things you gave to me." "It was one of those mother's treasured memories," says Sarah. "As I began to hook the piece, that memory came flooding back to me, and I knew that I wanted to dedicate and give the rug to Susan, who now has children of that age herself."

Sarah always strives to go beyond a photographic depiction while creating a rug. She planned the colors guided by not only the scene in the photograph but also the mood she wished to convey. She enjoyed using a variety of textures and values to give the water movement. To achieve this effect, she purchased spot-dyed, overdyed, and marbleized wool.

One of the challenges Sarah always had with prior projects was being able to find just the right fabric piece to achieve a particular look. For *All These Things*... she was thrilled to find a luminous spot-dyed piece of wool perfect for the sand. By working on this piece, Sarah learned a lot about hooking water, sand, and sky and found that each demanded its own technique.

All These Things ..., *25" x 19", #3-cut wool on linen, 2002.*

Hooking people has always been a challenge for Sarah, and she doesn't know if it's because the fabric strips are difficult to manipulate into the grid or if it's simply the pressure of hooking a likeness of those you know and love. "They can be our most critical audience," Sarah remarks.

Sarah gave the rug to her daughter, Susan, since it was the memory of her song that inspired the lovely piece. It's now being proudly displayed in Susan's living room in Santa Monica, California ... not too far from the ocean.

In the Judges' Words

"It's amazing the way the wind was captured."

"Particularly good cloud structure and interesting sand."

"Nice colors that blend very well ... the movement in the clouds is also quite impressive."

"Very realistic clouds and sky and nice movement in the water ... you can feel the sea breeze."

Antique Store in Plymouth

ORIGINAL DESIGNS

Fumiyo Hachisuka
Tokyo, Japan

Fumiyo Hachisuka lived in Canada from 1976 to 1983, and it was there that she first learned about rug hooking after seeing a flower bell pull displayed at the public library. Her background in dressmaking, quilting, and knitting prepared her for her new passion, and as she worked on her projects, she began teaching in Tokyo in an effort to introduce rug hooking to her country. "Recently, rug hooking is getting more popular than before, but still not many Japanese know exactly what it is," she explains. Fumiyo has completed more than 50 large and small rug projects and also teaches Chinese brush painting.

A few years ago, Fumiyo Hachisuka was attending the third conference of The International Guild of Handhooking Rugmakers in New Bedford, Massachusetts. After the conference, she slipped away to Plymouth to a hotel with a view of the seashore.

On the morning Fumiyo was to take a sightseeing trip to Boston, she woke up early, walked into town, and discovered the charming antique store now depicted in her rug. The store was not open, but its exterior enchanted this visitor from Japan. "I looked at the store from the outside," she recalls. "It was small but very curious. I took pictures, and I made a pattern from my sketch using the picture."

But Fumiyo did not rely solely on her photo and, being the creative person she is, incorporated some interesting features of her own. She added the rocking horse, the sheep, and the teddy bear in the toy cart that are pictured in front of the building and placed pieces of china behind the windowpane. These imaginary items made the work more interesting for her, she says, because she thought about what it would have been like for people to use these objects many years ago.

Her favorite part of the piece was being able to establish the ambience and atmosphere of a real antique store. Despite including items that weren't really there, she decided that her color planning would be as close a reproduction of the real store as possible. She spot and dip dyed new and recycled wool to match the colors on the building and hooked a small piece of white, gray, and black wool cloth to represent the letters on the paper tacked to the door.

The building has many straight lines, so getting a sense of perspective was Fumiyo's biggest challenge, particularly when it came to the building wall. "I used rug warp, and when I hooked the wall, the line was not in the right place," she says. "I tried to check my loops by hooking little by little."

Fumiyo rebuilt her house last year, and presently her rug is carefully wrapped in the attic, waiting for the day to be displayed.

In the Judges' Words

"A very complex design, but it's executed masterfully."

"I love how the building and other motifs run off the rug without being contained by a border."

"One of the most effective uses of perspective in the contest."

"It has a pleasant and warm feel that really draws the viewer in."

Antique Store in Plymouth, *29" x 37", #3-cut wool on rug warp, 2002.*

ORIGINAL DESIGNS

Bernice Howell
Beltsville, Maryland

When Bernice Howell retired from teaching in 1985, she wanted to use some of that free time to do something entirely different. She found rug hooking fulfilling and has completed about 50 pieces, with a preference for fine hooking with #3-cut wool. She also likes to do tapestry hooking because of the detail and color. Bernice often finds herself looking at objects and scenes with the possibility that they might make a good subject for a rug. She then relies on her husband's photography skills to capture the moment and uses that as her guide as she works on a project.

Best Friends

Bernice Howell prefers subjects that have special meaning to her as a way to preserve memories and loves turning photographs into wool masterpieces. After doing a hooked rug of her mother's portrait, it seemed like a natural next step to hook a picture of her brother, Jerry, and their dog on the back steps of their Minnesota farmhouse.

The photograph was taken in 1929, and because it was black-and-white, it gave Bernice the freedom to choose her own colors, relying a little on her recollections of the setting. She used mostly recycled wool, and any leftovers from the swatch she bought to hook her mother's face were used for her brother.

In fact, Bernice was never too far away from the portrait she had done of her mother as she hooked *Best Friends*. She kept it propped up in a chair beside her and studied it closely as her work progressed.

Bernice found that some parts of the hooking were fairly easy to do, and others were more challenging. The dog's fur, made up of a random collection of varied white stripes, tans, and grays, was fun and fairly easy, but her brother's head of tousled curls was more difficult. She wanted to avoid turning it into a solid-looking mass and ended up giving him four "hair cuts and regrowths" before she was satisfied with the results. "I ended up hooking loosely and letting the porch gray show through occasionally," she says. "Another big challenge was his coveralls. There was a lot of trial and error while trying to hook the folds and shadows."

Bernice was concerned about what effect constantly rolling and unrolling the rug would have on the integrity of the design, particularly to the intricacy of the faces. To finish off the rug, she secured museum-quality rag board onto a wood frame and stapled the excess monk's cloth to the back of the frame so that the rug on the front was permanently fastened as a framed picture.

Working on this project reinforced what Bernice already knew: If you want detail to be an integral part of what you're doing, you have to be very observant.

In the Judges' Words

"The gaze is gripping ... beautifully balanced in both color and value."

"The simple colors used in the piece make the overall appearance blend quite nicely."

"The face and hair on the child is absolutely stunning. It's very hard to achieve this look effectively."

"So animated!"

Best Friends, *16¹/₄" x 19¹/₂", #3-cut wool on linen, 2002.*

Bea Brock

Kerrville, Texas

Birds & Berries

Birds always captivated Bea Brock whenever she came upon them in a work of art. She loved the agility they displayed in the air and saw the delight they might lend to the overall effect of a rug she was already planning that incorporated vines and leaves.

As *Birds & Berries* came to life, however, Bea found her rug project growing ever larger. The rug project grew, not in size but in design, as she added berries to sustain her winged creatures ... and more berries to fill up the center diamond so that the image could be viewed from all sides.

"The flowing movement of the vines keeps the static repetition from dominating," she says, "Among the dance of the vines, I can almost hear the song of the birds."

Bea says the birds were initially a challenge, but that hooking them "was like dressing clowns for a circus." Her color choices for the birds became her favorite part of creating the rug. With some effort and the encouragement of teacher Jane Halliwell at the Star of Texas Rug Camp, Bea steered away from realistic depictions of the birds and just had fun. "I picked up variations on the colors throughout the rug by hooking the first bird with a wing one color, the tail another color, and the head another," she explains. "I decided that its partner across the rug from him would be done in the same colors but on different parts of the body. It was truly liberating to be able to mismatch these seemingly clownishly dressed birds."

Bea chose deep chocolate brown for the background and rough-dyed the leaves with teal combined with olive for interest. She tried several variations of teal for the border but then decided that it should comprise all the colors in the rug. She spotted some of the teal she had already dyed with intense red, gold, and olive, and mixed in leftovers from the vines. The border was then outlined with the leftover colors of the berries, gold on the inside border, and red and orange on the wavy outside border.

Bea's submission to *Celebration* marks the first juried competition she has ever entered, and her largest hooking challenge to date in the seven years she has been creating rugs. It took almost a year for Bea to complete *Birds & Berries* and, as with other projects she has done, she ponders how she would do it over again if she had the chance. "That's just the way hooking is for me," she remarks. "Every rug is a stepping stone to another idea, another color theme, another way of executing the details."

In the Judges' Words

"The overall design and use of color really keep the eye moving."

"This is an example of a great effect with a #8 cut—lots of subtle variations and just a great overall appearance."

"Great overall color balance and a clean, simple look."

"A nice, sophisticated primitive design."

Bea Brock's education and employment experience in graphic design more than prepared her for designing and hooking rugs. As she raised her family of four, she dabbled in quilting, sewing, painting, and other creative ventures. When her youngest enrolled in full-day kindergarten, Bea went in search of a more challenging creative outlet. Rug hooking filled the bill, and she began creating and developing new patterns. The local shop where Bea first learned to hook rugs accepted several of her designs and made them into kits. Bea has taught in a needlework shop, in her home, and at the First Annual Angela Pumphrey Workshop in San Antonio.

Birds & Berries, *46" x 62¹/₂", #8-cut wool on linen, 2002.*

ORIGINAL DESIGNS

Lynne Fowler
Westover, Maryland

Lynne Fowler is a fiber artist in the truest sense of the word. Armed with a BFA from Moore College of Art, she has been a weaver, spinner, knitter, and quilter but now considers rug hooking her profession. She likes to work with anywhere from a #3 to an 8½ cut of wool, loves playing with color, and admits that some days she will go into her studio and "play in the dye pots." To date, she has completed 28 rugs and "zillions" of smaller pieces and exhibits her work at local art galleries and museums. She is a McGown-certified teacher, a member of the Association of Traditional Hooking Artists and The International Guild of Handhooking Rugmakers, and co-director of the Delmarva Workshop.

L ynne Fowler's heartfelt rug, simply titled *Floyd*, has an equally heartfelt story to accompany it. The starving, hairless, and abandoned dog arrived at her doorstep after the hurricane of the same name.

Lynne had decided years ago that she didn't want to have any more dogs after her aged poodle died. But Floyd had other plans, she says, and the sad-eyed pooch "wormed his way into our hearts." Lynne, who has been hooking rugs for seven years, got the idea to do a wool recreation of Floyd while attending the Delmarva Workshop. She felt that it would make the perfect Christmas gift for her husband.

Lynne began the project by taking several photos of the dog and scanning them into her computer for enlargement. After transferring the photo to linen, she tackled the dyeing and tried many different formulas to achieve the colors she wanted for his coat. "I have brackish well water, so my dyeing can be very unpredictable," Lynne says. "Oddly enough, the most challenging part of the rug was the grassy background. I took all of my leftover greens and simmered them with onion skins. I then divided the wool into light, medium, and dark piles."

Floyd was Lynne's first experience hooking animals, and she learned to approach the design in terms of values and sections. She says that her favorite part of the rug is Floyd's eyes and was told by her workshop teacher, Elizabeth Black, that occasionally an animal's

FLOYD

FOUND STARVING AND BALD COVERED WITH FLEAS

NOW HE IS LIVING A LIFE OF EASE

Floyd, *41" x 30 1/2", #3- and 4-cut wool on linen, 2002.*

eyes will follow you around the room. "I think Floyd's eyes do that," she remarks.

Lynne's original intent to present the rug to her husband as a holiday gift has been waylaid for now. She has been too busy putting it on exhibit at the Maryland Shores Rug School, the McGown National Show, and the Art Institute and Gallery in Salisbury, Maryland. But she hasn't been that busy that she couldn't take in another stray. Lynne recently added another abandoned dog, Lady, to her household. No doubt Lady will soon be the subject of another beautiful rug.

In the Judges' Words

"*The background has just enough interest without overriding the subject.*"

"*The dog's face has so much character!*"

"*Great lettering.*"

"*The dog looks like he's ready to stand up and walk toward the viewer ... well done! The eyes are also spectacular.*"

ORIGINAL DESIGNS

Linda Rae Coughlin
Warren, New Jersey

Fiber art has been a part of Linda Rae Coughlin's life for as long as she can remember. As a child, her grandmother taught her how to sew her own clothes, crochet, and punch hook rugs. But it was Linda's first rug hooking teacher, Lorraine Williams, who encouraged her to have her own voice and grow in her art. Linda belongs to a few artist groups outside rug hooking, and one of her goals is to have rug hooking recognized as an art form and exhibited in galleries and museums. Her work has been depicted in several publications, including A Passion for the Creative Life: Textiles That Lift the Spirit, *and she was a judge for a past* Celebration *annual.*

Fly Oh Fly

Just ask Linda Rae Coughlin to compare rug hooking and art, and she'll tell you they are one and the same. That's exactly how she saw *Fly Oh Fly,* one in a series of pictorial rugs she is in the process of creating.

Linda's work in the series is loosely based on self-portraits inspired by her own and other women's issues and incorporating words and symbols that have spiritual or emotional meaning. For Linda, birds represent freedom and a sense of adventure and were an appropriate choice as an artistic subject.

"When they are flying, they are always seeing from another perspective," she says. "I really like using symbolism in my pieces and love adding other elements that are both visually stimulating and push me to expand in my approach to my art."

Linda's desire to take her rug hooking to another level was the impetus for this project, and she was fearless when it came to incorporating new techniques that would challenge her despite 13 years of rug hooking experience. One of those techniques involved the use of materials normally viewed as foreign to fiber art. She appliquéd wool fabric and recycled sweaters to the linen foundation to make the bird's head and wings and sewed on a piece of felt for the ground that the bird is standing on. The bird's legs were also appliquéd on with overdyed ultra suede. She then added hand-dyed feathers and beads.

Another challenge that awaited Linda was finishing edges that were not in the traditional rectangular, round, or oval shape. Instead, Linda created edges that were an outline of a bird's wing. Getting the rug to hang correctly because of its unconventional form was yet another challenge for Linda.

Linda says she likes to look at life with new eyes, and just like the birds that soar effortlessly through the sky, *Fly Oh Fly* has taken her to new heights. This year, the piece was exhibited at the American Folk Art Museum in New York City during their first annual "Rug Day."

In the Judges' Words

"This rug really draws you in and makes you stay. A great subtle use of other media."

"An effective use of additional materials. The finishing around the tricky edge is quite good."

"I love the use of other stitching techniques, appliqué, and embellishing."

Fly Oh Fly, *23" x 39", #4- through 7-cut wool on linen, 2002.*

PHOTOGRAPH COURTESY OF LINDA RAE COUGHLIN

CELEBRATION XIII

ORIGINAL DESIGNS

Karen Balon

Goffstown, New Hampshire

Karen Balon's obsession with rug hooking began in 1992 when she observed a demonstration at the League of New Hampshire Craftsmen's annual fair. Since then, she has hooked 18 pieces, including rugs, pillows, coasters, and wallhangings. She is now a juried member of the league where her obsession began. She is also a member of the national and local Association of Traditional Hooking Artists and owns Art in the Wool, where she sells her original rug projects along with commissioned works. Although she is self-taught, Karen seeks the expertise of her fellow fiber artists to learn all she can about her passion. "I feel I've transitioned from making rugs to creating pieces of art," she says.

The Girls

Karen Balon had a burning desire to tackle something different in the craft of rug hooking. She wanted to steer away from commercial patterns and develop one of her own designs, as well as focus on her favorite subject matter—people.

Karen didn't have to look any further than her own family members to gather inspiration. "I had taken a picture of my three nieces and decided that this photo would be the piece to hook," she remarks.

The click of the camera, however, proved to be much easier than actually capturing *The Girls* in wool. With her usual attention to detail, Karen searched for just the right flesh formula, as she would be dyeing most of her wool. When she couldn't find just what she was looking for, she contacted Connie Charleson for formulas that had been mentioned in a previous *Celebration* issue.

Karen adapted the colors by using the jar dyeing method until she was able to attain the desired shades. She then scanned the photo, enlarged it, printed it out, and traced

The Girls, *36" x 18", #2- and 3-cut wool on monk's cloth, 2002.*

over it with red dot before she transferred it onto a monk's cloth backing.

After the dyeing was completed for the background and the girls, Karen finally was ready to hook. She enjoyed bringing out the expressions and uniqueness of each face, but hooking the girls' necks proved to be her biggest challenge. Karen found herself doing more pulling out and re-hooking then she had imagined.

"In the picture I had taken of the girls, their necks were covered, so I would sit there feeling my own neck, where the high points and crevasses were, and then try to hook what I was feeling," Karen says. "After awhile, I finally remembered that I had an anatomy book for drawing human bodies and got that out to use as a reference as well."

Karen's five months of work paid off in a big way. *The Girls* received both first place and "Best in Show" at last year's Deerfield Fair and is now proudly displayed in Karen's foyer inside her New Hampshire home.

Those smiling faces continue to captivate their creator more than any framed photograph or painted portrait. "I would have to say the girls' eyes are my favorite," Karen explains. "I just feel like they are communicating with me whenever I look at them."

In the Judges' Words

"Uniquely photographic ... this is a wonderful use of values to make the flesh 'work.'"

"Lovely background work."

"This piece makes me want to meet these nice ladies."

CELEBRATION XIII

ORIGINAL DESIGNS

Lana Roske
Vestal, New York

In the 22 years since she accepted a friend's invitation to observe a rug hooking class, Lana Roske has tried just about every hooking style imaginable. "I have hooked Orientals, pictorials, and primitive designs," she says. "I have completed about 60 pieces of varied commercial designs, originals, and adaptations." Lana says the craft, as well as the people she has met through her rug hooking activities, have enhanced her life in so many ways. Her husband and daughter support her hooking passion, and even her two grandsons have requested personalized rugs. Lana's work has appeared in three previous editions of A Celebration of Hand-Hooked Rugs.

Haitian Farmers

Lana Roske almost missed the opportunity to take a photograph that served as the inspiration for her next rug hooking project. *Haitian Farmers* depicts a group of farm workers that passed by the guesthouse where Lana and her group were staying while in Haiti.

"Our purpose was to assist in the construction of the second floor of a school in the village of Verrettes and to interact with the Haitian people," she says. "One morning, we saw a group of farmers walking out to the fields with their primitive hoes over their shoulders. No one had a camera at the time, but late in the afternoon we happened to catch them returning to the village. They posed for us as they passed by the guest house." Lana had been looking for a subject for her next rug and immediately hoped the photo would be something she could use as subject matter.

When Lana got home, she developed the photograph, but it was underexposed and the farmers seemed small. Her son was able to enhance it with a computer program, and an enlargement was made.

Lana sought the assistance of Pris Buttler at the Castle in the Clouds Rug School, who helped in the development of the pattern's design. Lana's original plan was to hook the shirts in light colors and do the leaves and grasses in a variety of greens, but Pris encouraged her to use darker colors for the shirts and use light, medium, and dark greens in a variety of textures for the banana and other leaves. "It took a bit of convincing for me to accept darker, richer colors, since my memory of Haiti had been that of heat and bright sun," Lana remarks.

Lana was also worried about accurately capturing the facial details of the farmers. But Pris again came to the rescue by suggesting the use of lights and darks for this part of the rug. Lana adds that she dyed a light blue-gray for the background and found a darker blue-gray that worked perfectly for the border.

Lana has no regrets about following her teacher's recommendations. Pris taught her that the use of lights and darks helps in color planning, offers contrast to move the eye, and sets off certain items in the rug. Lana also felt less pressure about trying to accomplish the reality of the scene and focused more on the artistic value of the piece.

Haitian Farmers now hangs in the church office where Lana works. She recently returned to Haiti and purchased a metal cut-out of a Haitian farmer, which complements the piece quite nicely.

Haitian Farmers, *40" x 22", #4-cut wool on linen, 2002.*

In the Judges' Words

"The complicated foreground and quiet background give the overall piece excellent balance."

"The color is spectacular, and I like the simplicity of the design."

"A great use of color and wonderful balance in this piece. The scene really suggests a story ... I want to know more about where these guys are going."

"It's amazing how these pictorial visual elements actually create a pattern!"

Machias Seal Island

CELEBRATION XIII

ORIGINAL DESIGNS

Trish Johnson
Fergus, Ontario

Trish Johnson was a university student who began rug hooking after visiting her aunt. "She was hooking a rug of a sailing ship, and I spent a week hooking the sky for her," says Trish. "Many years later, I bought a Rittermere-Hurst-Field kit at the One of a Kind Show in Toronto and have been hooking ever since." Trish is a graduate of the Ontario College of Art, has attended Burlington Rug Hooking School, and is working on her teacher certification from the Ontario Hooking Craft Guild. She enjoys working with her hands and the slow pace of hooking a rug.

T rish Johnson likes doing pictorial rugs of landscapes that have special meaning for her. *Machias Seal Island* is no exception. The rug is filled with family memories, family words, and a bit of mystery for the observer. "My grandmother lived on Machias Seal Island," Trish explains. "Her father was the lighthouse keeper. She met Jim Balmer, captain of the *Clayola*, when he was delivering a load of coal. She married him and had three daughters, one of whom was my mother."

Trish made the journey there in the summer of 2000 with the desire to document the places important to her family's history. This avid rug hooker knew of no better way to preserve that history than using wool.

Trish loved designing the rug and decided that across the early morning sky, she would hook a page from her grandmother's diary and replicate her grandmother's handwriting, along with her idiosyncratic use of "u's" instead of "n's". "You have to work at it to read it," admits Trish. "I have kept some mystery in it by deliberately letting some words drift behind things. I wanted the effect of superimposing a page of my grandmother's diary on lined paper without the sky appearing to be striped. The text interested me as pattern and color and not just as content."

PHOTOGRAPH BY JOSEPH BERGEL KITCHENER, ONTARIO, CANADA

Machias Seal Island, *37" x 27", #4- and 5-cut wool and yarn on linen, 2002.*

This was Trish's first try at hooking handwriting, and it was that aspect of the rug that turned out to be the greatest challenge. She ended up hooking much of the sky twice but learned that combining text with image added interest to the work.

Trish used a combination of recycled wool for the shingled roofs and used lopi natural wool for the milkweed in among the grasses. She enjoyed putting whipping around the edges and continuing the picture over the border.

Machias Seal Island is part of a series being developed by Trish that reflects her family's past. For her, however, the rug not only depicts a place and tells part of a story but is also an artistic arrangement of complementary colors. The rug was exhibited at the Wellington County Museum and Archives in the Insights show, where it received the Elora Fabric Award.

In the Judges' Words

"*A unique and successful technique in layering the letters, then grasses, then the scene.*"

"*The overall design and color is great. The words add so much without taking away from the design.*"

"*Good shading in the house, and the grass has a lot of interest.*"

"*A difficult task executed perfectly.*"

CELEBRATION XIII

ORIGINAL DESIGNS

Matthew and Andrew at Moose Pond

Judy Fresk
Glastonbury, Connecticut

Judy Fresk made the natural transition from sewing, knitting, and other types of fiber art to rug hooking after seeing a one-woman rug show inside her town's historical society museum. Her retirement in 1992 was the perfect opportunity to learn the art, and she has since completed 24 rugs and teaches a class in rug hooking. Her rugs have been featured in previous editions of A Celebration of Hand-Hooked Rugs, Good Housekeeping Crafts magazine, and by the Wadsworth Atheneum in Hartford, Connecticut, the oldest continuing museum in the United States, in their exhibit, "Hooking: Folk Art to Fiber Art." Judy is a member of the Association of Traditional Hooking Artists and the McGown Guild.

Matthew and Andrew at Moose Pond holds a multitude of memories for its creator Judy Fresk. This family vacation spot located in Bridgeton, Maine, was for years a favorite retreat—first for Judy's parents in the 1950s and then for Judy's own growing family. "But as life will have it, when my children were in high school, we stopped our yearly vacation," she recalls. "Then the idea of a return visit began to develop. My parents, my brother and his children, and my children with their children were all there."

Judy used her camera to capture this unique gathering of four generations. Over the next three years, she would look at one of the photos depicting her two grandsons, ages two and four at the time, and thought it would make a wonderful subject for a rug. Judy's decision to hook the rug, however, was not based solely on how much she liked the photograph: She hooked it because she knew it would present hooking challenges she had never experienced before.

Judy did the drawing, color planning, and dyeing of new wool using spot dyes for the trees, paintbrush dyeing for the sky, swatches for the children, and dip dyes for the sand. This marked the first time in her more than 10 years of rug making that she tackled human faces and bodies, and it was those aspects of the rug that turned out to be the most challenging for her. But once the piece was completed, she was delighted with the boys' likeness and knew she had succeeded when one of the boys recognized the face of his brother. "I knew I didn't have to make any more changes," she says proudly. "Hooking this rug really taught me how to look at a photo or picture and hook just what I see."

Judy finished *Matthew and Andrew at Moose Pond* by using a 3" strip of wool over a piece of cording. She plans on hanging the rug on the wall inside her studio but hopes to one day to present it as a gift to her son. "I will always look at this rug and remember our wonderful week on Moose Pond," she says.

Matthew and Andrew at Moose Pond, *33" x 33¹/2", #3- through 6-cut wool on linen, 2002.*

In the Judges' Words

"I love the wonderful clear and bright colors, as well as the way the impressionistic trees show light and shadow. Perfectly accentuates the mood of a happy day for the boys."

"Great trees!"

"The color change in the receding shoreline brings amazing depth to the piece."

"This rug has absolutely beautiful perspective."

ORIGINAL DESIGNS

Sally D'Albora
Rockville, Maryland

In 1990, Sally D'Albora's braiding teacher of 10 years encouraged the class to attend Green Mountain Rug School, and it was there that Sally became enthralled with the craft. Since then, she has completed 20 large rugs and 12 small pieces and likes to do her own hand-cutting using narrow and wide to very wide strips for her work. Sally lectures to small groups, teaches occasionally, and has attended the Buckeystown Country Workshop numerous times. She is a member of the Association of Traditional Hooking Artists, a judge at the Maryland State Fair, and has garnered many awards. She was a finalist in Celebration IV *and a judge for* Celebration XII.

New Life

Sally D'Albora grew up around the Chesapeake Bay area, and her intrigue with the locale inspired her in 1994 to begin hooking a series of designs that pays tribute to this beautiful Maryland waterway. *New Life* is the fourth in that series and portrays the verdant surroundings and the creatures that call this place home. "The wildlife is fascinating to watch, study, and in some cases, like the blue crab, a delight to consume," she says. "I never tire of the beautiful bay."

Sally's approach to color planning was the same as for her past projects. She started by pulling the colors she needed from her wool bank, which are dyed using spot, dip, casserole, and other techniques. As her work progressed, she realized she would have to take into account how light rebounded off the different objects appearing in the scene she was creating, particularly the turtle. She used yarn in many areas to exaggerate color and reflection and worked on each segment of the turtle, taking into consideration how the light reflected on the large turtle's top, sides, and bottom areas.

Sally says that her favorite part of the rug is the group of eggs in various stages of hatching. She incorporated seven young turtles in the piece, some of which remain close by their mother while others wander off in different directions.

One big challenge for Sally came about as a result of her utilizing a large amount of the color green to develop the leaves and grasses. She was careful, she says, to make certain that the color did not conceal or dominate the other motifs, particularly the large turtle.

It took Sally nine months to complete *New Life*, which she finished by whipping the edge with a color similar to the outside hooked edge. She then added a piece of flannel, instead of tape, to cover the raw edge of the backing.

Sally hopes to continue her fascination with the Chesapeake Bay through more hooked work, and while she has not decided on a permanent place in her home to display her rug, its brilliant flora and fauna are sure to bring new life to any space she chooses.

PHOTOGRAPH COURTESY OF SALLY D'ALBORA

New Life, *52" x 28", hand-cut wool flannel and wool yarn on linen, 2002.*

In the Judges' Words

"Where do I begin? What a masterful use of color and value ... it's impressionistic and gives great movement to the piece. At the same time, it's balanced, gently urging you into the piece to stay, look around, and get mucky. The piece really makes you think about the balance of life, and how the food chain and life is much like a tapestry."

"It takes a great mind to include all this detail in a rug successfully!"

"Very effective use of color ... just a striking piece all around."

"So much is going on in this rug ... amazing!"

Our Fiftieth

ORIGINAL DESIGNS

Alma G. Synakowski
Utica, New York

Fabric and art have always been a big part of Alma G. Synakowski's life for as long as she can remember. She majored in textiles while in college and took as many fine and applied arts courses as she could. Although she worked in commercial illustration for part of her professional life, she never lost her interest in fabric and design. When the opportunity arose to take classes in rug hooking and braiding in 1963, Alma dove into the challenge with enthusiasm. "The very first day of class was the beginning of a wonderful and exciting adventure, beginning my lifelong interest in both braiding and hooking," she says.

A lma G. Synakowski felt that her 50th wedding anniversary celebration in Vermont, her birthplace, needed more than a collection of snapshots, videotapes, and souvenirs to serve as memories. The Wilburton Inn in Manchester and the Arlington Inn in Arlington became the focal points for the weekend gathering, and Alma wanted to record it in her own special way.

For this rug hooker of 40 years, that meant creating a wool masterpiece depicting the joyous family event set against the beautiful vistas and mountainside. "I tried to incorporate this beauty and excitement into something of an heirloom piece that everyone might take turns sharing and enjoying," she says. "Every time the family came to visit, they had to check on its progress. Now they want to take turns borrowing it for their homes."

Alma created a montage of some of the many photographs that were snapped during the weekend and found it a challenge to include the detail she wanted on a small 27" x 20" piece of monk's cloth. She used #3-cut wool and then embroidery wool for the smallest flowers and hooked in the postures and gestures of family members. "Making each individual personality recognizable required patience, and it was of particular importance to me to have the two large buildings as architecturally accurate, well-proportioned, and detailed as possible," she says. Alma adds that balancing shapes, sizes, colors, values, and textures became an ongoing learning process as her work progressed.

Alma has always enjoyed dyeing her own wool, but she did some experimenting for *Our Fiftieth* to achieve the variety of greens in the lawn and field expanses. Particularly challenging to her was the water, as she wanted to capture its movement as well as its color in shades of blue and the characteristic aqua of swimming pools.

Alma included many elements of the design in order to personalize the piece, such as showing her husband taking a picture of her as she sat on the steps of the terrace, and her grandchildren playing in the pool. But the relatively small size of her "canvas" taught her to avoid adding distracting details that might clutter and weaken the composition.

The framing of *Our Fiftieth* was put on hold while Alma took a respite from the New York winter and went to Florida. But she already envisions what the frame will look like. She says it will be gold. For a rug honoring her golden anniversary, what other color could it be?

Our Fiftieth, *27" x 20",*
#3-cut wool on monk's
cloth, 2002.

In the Judges' Words

"The colors, design, and overall subject matter really work in this rug!"

"A very complex design that is beautifully hooked."

"This is a busy piece, but it works because it has very nice balance."

"Joyful and active ... what fun it is to ponder all those family activities."

Paper Dolls

CELEBRATION XIII

ORIGINAL DESIGNS

Denise Reithofer
Burlington, Ontario

Denise Reithofer was viewing a group of rug hookers at a 1995 harvest festival and was immediately captivated by what she saw. She was attracted to the art's portability and its capacity to use recycled material. A year later, she searched for the tools and materials she needed to get started and got to work on her first project. To date, she has completed 11 pieces. "I draw elements from each style of hooking I encounter and apply them to my original designs," she says. Denise is a teaching assistant in fiber art at a Waldorf school and a member of The International Guild of Hand-hooking Rugmakers, the Ontario Hooking Craft Guild, and two community rug hooking guilds.

A rug hooker never knows what they might come out with and what new lessons they might learn when they participate in a workshop. In Denise Reithofer's case, she walked away with a new and innovative idea for a rug hooking project.

Denise got the inspiration for *Paper Dolls* in a workshop on doll sculpting in fabric that she took with a Toronto artist. She already knew about the endless possibilities in design that hooking afforded her through her seven years as a rug hooker and from past workshop leaders that encouraged her to be original in her thinking and design.

Along with all of this was a maternal grandfather who worked in oils and etching and her university degree in art history and painting. This supplied Denise with a vast array of knowledge in other creative fields of study.

Denise used new and recycled wool on burlap backing to create the innovative *Paper Dolls*. She finished the piece by whipping the turned frontward edges with wool yarn, so she could eliminate the need for bias tape.

Her favorite part of working on the rug was the internal design and color of each doll, as she found it fun to make it up as she went along. "I did all the color planning and dyed

Paper Dolls, *65" x 49", #4-cut wool on burlap, 2001.*

wherever needed," she says.

Denise says it took sheer perseverance to complete the background for *Paper Dolls*, an aspect of the rug that she says was the most challenging. But that determination has paid off, as the light-colored backdrop serves to highlight and contrast the diverse designs worn by the three dolls. The piece won first place in a juried show and exhibition show and was selected by Jessie A. Turbayne for inclusion in her fourth rug hooking book.

Paper Dolls has a permanent place in Denise's studio and is a constant reminder of her own creativity and originality, as well as proof that anything is possible in rug hooking.

In the Judges' Words

---

*"Intriguing subject matter ...
very complex."*

---

*"The expertise shown in the execution of
this abstract design is superlative."*

---

*"A creative use of design that is pulled
off with fantastic color choices."*

---

*"Very original and
technically impressive."*

CELEBRATION XIII
ORIGINAL DESIGNS

Pat Merikallio
New Canaan, Connecticut

Pat Merikallio acquired an interest in rug hooking when a friend was beginning to teach and persuaded her to give it a try. She took her friend's advice and has been hooking and designing her own rugs since 1978. Pat has tried almost all the techniques, but after completing more than 50 rug hooking projects, she says she prefers using wide cuts. Her work has appeared in five prior editions of A Celebration of Hand-Hooked Rugs *and was exhibited at the Wenham Museum. Her rugs have also won "Best in Show" at the New England State Fair and the Cahoon Museum. She belongs to the Association of Traditional Hooking Artists and the McGown Guild.*

The Sea Otters

P at Merikallio is a former fashion designer who was accustomed to coordinating color, texture, and form to attain a unique sense of style. Once she got involved in rug hooking, she used her fashion know-how and artistic talents in helping her design over 50 rugs in the past 25 years, some of which have won "Best in Show" awards and blue ribbons.

It is no surprise then that Pat's decision to make a rug for one of her twin grandsons necessitated doing some investigation: She had to make sure her arrangement made sense, and all the motifs and creatures connected in some way. "They live in California in a small town on the Pacific Ocean, so I thought this rug should be about the sea," explains Pat. "I decided to hook the sea otters because they are so loveable, and so I did some research."

In her research, Pat determined that sea otters swim exclusively on their backs, and when they want to sleep, they wrap themselves in kelp vines to keep from floating out to sea. Pat also discovered what sea otters like to eat and hooked those items—including an octopus and a starfish—along the border. She says that one of the most challenging parts of this rug was relating the border back to the center of the rug.

Pat planned the colors of her original design and dyed new and recycled wool using spot, dip, and casserole techniques, as well as painting some wool. One of the color-related challenges she faced was the desire to give the impression of gray animals by using every color except gray. Pat loved playing with all the different colors she created for *The Sea Otters* and seeing the role those colors eventually had in bringing this small part of the sea to life. To finish off the piece, she whipped around the edges and used tape to cover the raw edge.

Pat likes the fact that the rug can be viewed from any direction, as long as the observer doesn't mind an upside-down octopus. She now plans on hooking a rug for each of her five grandchildren.

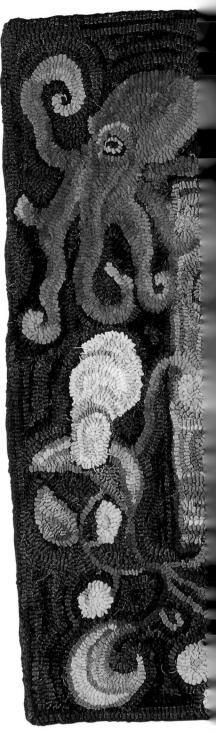

The Sea Otters, *36" x 28",*
#6-cut wool on linen, 2002.

"Beautifully 'transcolor' dyed wools and a bold use of color and value. It's nice that she's not afraid to use #6-cut whiskers."

"This border works quite well, as it trails into the background of the rug."

"The colors really pull this piece together, and I love the border."

"This rug is an example of color mastery: It absolutely sparkles!"

Cynthia (Cindi) Gay
Pemberville, Ohio

Cindi Gay began hooking after seeing a demonstration on a television show. She quickly fell in love with the rich colors and practical utility of making rugs. In the past three years she has completed five large rugs, a vest, a footstool, several wallhangings, pillows, and small pieces. She teaches classes in her home, through community education, and at a needlework shop in Toledo. Cindi prefers hooking pictorials and this year completed her first commission that memorialized a neighbor's childhood farm. "After it was completed, she said, 'It looks just like I remember it,'" Cindi says. "That was the best compliment she could have given."

Village of Pemberville

Cindi Gay fell in love with the historical buildings in Pemberville, Ohio, after moving there about 10 years ago. The night before she was to begin a design class at the Sauder Village rug camp, she dashed into town and took photographs of some buildings in the hopes they would serve as a guide for her next rug project. "As luck would have it, the weather was not the best for snapping photos," she recalls. "With an umbrella wedged under my arm and resting on my head, I held the camera with both hands, leaned back to get the umbrella out of the shot, and took pictures."

The difficult balancing act may have been a precursor for the obstacles that were to follow. She was hooking the rug for a month without a color plan and came to a point where she needed to decide where she was going and what she needed to dye. "I immediately figured out what was bothering me," Cindi says. "All the rich deep reds were on the same side of the rug. Luckily, rug warp has two sides, so I removed the hooking, flipped it over, and tediously redrew the pattern."

Cindi traveled almost two hours each way to get expert advice from her teacher. During each session the pair would hang the rug over the blackboard and critique it. The experience proved to be invaluable because it gave Cindi a sense of the detail and depth needed to create a successful piece.

Cindi tried various combinations of color, cut, texture, and direction of hooking. She used spot dyes to achieve the buildings' bricks and give the illusion of clapboards. She also used spot dyes, textures, and some solids arranged from light to dark. She drove two hours each way to buy the wool for the border. When the shop did not have enough of it, she drove back the next week when they received more.

Cindi feels that all her efforts have been well worth it, as she honed her pictorial skills on this rug. "The struggle I went through to master the grass, sky, and pine trees was worth the time," she explains. "The elements that I thought would be difficult turned out to be the simplest." Cindi has been amazed at the response to this rug. The comments she likes best, however, are from those who say this rug inspired them to try their own pictorial.

In the Judges' Words

"Very nice use of shadow and light."

"Exceptional! Attention to detail is wonderful … the fine detail, the perspective, the shadow on the barrel against the house … it's all great! The farmland in the background gives the entire piece tremendous depth."

"The border frames this scene in just the right way."

"The colors are rich and well-balanced, and the motifs have such great detail. The soft sky gives the whole rug a very soft feel. I also love the interesting and unique shape of the rug."

Village of Pemberville, *36" x 60", multiple cuts of wool on rug warp, 2002.*

RUG HOOKING RESOURCES

A PRIMITIVE PASTIME
N4 W22496 Bluemound Rd, Waukesha, WI 53186
(262) 513–9056

Over 900 sq. ft. of patterns, kits, wools, books and equipment for rug hooking, appliqué, penny rugs and other "primitive pastimes"

Shop online at:
www.justalittlebitcountry.com

"Log Cabin Rug Hooking Designs" by Kari

Full color catalogs $5.00

ASILOMAR RUG SCHOOL
February 29 – March 5, 2004

- **Experienced McGown Instructors**
- **Classes taught in both fine cut and primitive**

Contact: Basha Quilici
(415) 488-9533

E-mail: hvinterior@aol.com

Best's Harbour Rug Hooking
Supplies • Classes • Workshops • Catalogue
519 Main Street, Williams, ON, Canada L7G 3T1
(905) 702-8311
www.bestsharbour.com • info@bestsharbour.com

CAMBRIA PINES RUG CAMP
Cambria, California
June 6–11, 2004

Seven Great Teachers

Contact Gene Shepherd
108 N. Vine, Anaheim, CA 92805
(714) 956-5150
goodshepherd53@juno.com

Castle In The Clouds
Rug Hooking Creations

29th Annual Seminar Lookout Mountain
Rug Hooking Supplies—Wetter than Wet Wool & Patterns
Fleecewood & Designs by Debbie
Designs by Ramona Maddox—Tapestry Bags

Ramona Maddox
7108 Panavista Lane, Chattanooga, TN 37421
(423) 892–1858
Castlerug@comcast.net

39th Year of
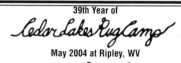
Cedar Lakes Rug Camp

May 2004 at Ripley, WV

For more info send SASE to:
Billie Jean Glass

E-mail: billiejean glass@aol.com

SUMMER ADDRESS:	WINTER ADDRESS:
2100 Island Drive	8144 Pine Circle
Lexington, KY 40502	Tamarac, FL 33321
859-269-3818	954-726-5824

European Wool
Textures...Plaids...Colors...Overdyes
Call or Send $3.00 for a Swatch List
Country Gatherings
Tricia Travis
18771 FM 2252
San Antonio, Texas 78266
210-651-4470
countrygatherings@mail.com

CROSS CREEK FARM RUG HOOKING SCHOOL
(April 25–30, 2004)
and
RUG HOOKING STUDIO
13440 Taylor Wells Road
Chardon, Ohio 44024
(440) 635–0209

Supplies for hooking, proddy, penny rugs, braiding; introductory instruction.
Source for Katherine Porter Patterns.
By Appointment Only • Beth Croup, Owner

THE DORR MILL STORE

P.O. Box 88 • Guild, NH 03754

Manufacturers of permanently moth-proofed fine wools for hooking and braiding since 1962.
TOLL FREE: 1-800-846-DORR
e-mail: dorrmillstore@sugar.river.nct.

GRUBER'S LAP HOOP
Perfect for Hooking
Rotates, swivels, locks in any position

P.O. Box 87
Pierz, MN 56364

(320) 468-6553
Check out the Hoop at:
www.grubersquiltshop.com

HALCYON YARN

Rug Yarn in 3 styles
& OVER 175 COLORS
Hooking & Punching Supplies

12 SCHOOL ST / BATH, ME / 04530
1-800-341-0282 / www.halcyonyarn.com

HANGIN' ROUND DYE SPOONS
Connie Bradley
18550 Pitts Rd.
Wellington, OH 44090
(440) 647-2473
E-mail: connie@tape-inc.com

ALUMINUM DYE SPOONS
$1/128$ tsp. up to 1 tsp.
Set of 8 Spoons
$50.00/set-ppd plus $3.50 S&H.

HARRY M. FRASER CO.

Jeanette Szatkowski
433 Duggins Road
Stoneville, NC 27048

(336) 573-9830
(336) 573-3545 FAX

Jesta Hooker at Heart

E-mail:fraserrugs@aol.com
Web: www.fraserrugs.com

Complete line of hooking and braiding supplies. Cloth Slitting Machines

---

Hartman's Hook
Primitive Hooked Rugs

Hartman Hooks
Rigby Cutters
dyed wool

Cindy Hartman

P.O. Box 938
Hudson, Ohio 44236
(330) 653-9730
hhooks@mac.com

Heart in Hand Rug Hooking, Inc.

P.O. Box 8117
Glen Ridge, NJ 07028

1-800-290-5242
CALL FOR A FREE CATALOG

RUG HOOKING RESOURCES

HOOKED TREASURES

Cherylyn Brubaker
6 Iroquois Circle
Brunswick, ME 04011
(207) 729–1380
(207) 729-1380
Pattern Catalog $5 ppd
Classes and Supplies
NEW! Expanded Studio

THE HOUSE OF PRICE, INC
177 BRICKYARD ROAD
MARS, PA 16046-3001

CHARCO — PRIMCO PATTERNS

Toll free- 1-877-RUG-HOOK
Facsimile- 1-724-625-0178
E-mail- rughook@sgi.net

JACQUELINE DESIGNS

Jacqueline Hansen
237 Pine Point Road
Scarborough, ME 04074

(207) 883-5403
www.rughookersnetwork.com

Design Catalog, Workshops,
Supplies, Kits
and Custom Design

LIZIANA CREATIONS

Shop located at
515 John Fitch Blvd., Rt. 5
South Windsor, CT 06074
860 290-8619

Complete Rug Hooking Supplier
Custom Dyeing & Designing
Catalogue of Patterns
Lessons

Montair Homespun/Ann Wrenn
120 Montair Ct.
Danville, CA 94526-3724

Fanciful, three-dimension
primitive
holiday pattern designs

Color brochure $3.00
1-925-743-8354
E-mail: montairhomespun@yahoo.com

Northwoods Wool

ORIGINAL PRIMITIVE DESIGNS
KITS, PATTERNS & HAND-DYED WOOL
CATALOG & WOOL SAMPLES $6.00
P.O. Box 1027
Cumberland, WI 54829
(715) 822-3198
www.northwoodswool.com

THE OLIVE BRANCH

HAND HOOKED RUG STUDIO

Andrea Trout
P.O. Box 181
Portsmouth, RI 02871

(401) 683-0849
E-mail: attrout@cs.com

CLASSES • SUPPLIES • HAND-DYED WOOLS

On The Ocean
Rug Hooking
Conference
JANUARY 16–21, 2004

The Sea Turtle Inn, Jacksonville, Florida

For information contact: Judy Colley
2451 Michael, SW,
Wyoming, MI 49509
(616) 531-9255 • E-mail: *rcjumar@aol.com*

PINE ISLAND
primitives

Classes and Patterns
Catalog $6.00 ppd.
Sally Kallin
861 Balsam Court, NE
Pine Island, MN 55963
(507) 356-2908
E-mail: rugs@pitel.net

PRIMITIVE PASTIMES

Kim Dubay
410 Walnut Hill Road
N. Yarmouth, ME
04097

(207) 829-3725
Original hooked rug kits,
patterns and supplies.

We offer a complete line of
Hooking Designs and Supplies
Order our *"Book of Designs"*
Call us at 1-800-268-9813
www.LetsHookRugs.com

THE ROBIN'S NEST
Studio of Traditional
Rug Hooking

Instruction • Supplies • Accessories
Online Catalog • Newsletter

robinsnest@kerrlake.com
www.kerrlake.com/robinest
Robin D. Hasty, 2359 Highway 58
Buffalo Junction, VA 24529

(434) 374–5830 • (434) 374–HOOK

ROCK RIVER
RUGGERS CAMP
Oregon, Illinois (Rockford Area)
Come play hooky with us!

October 10–15, 2004

J. Reckwerdt / J. Podlasek
20688 Nicolette Drive
Bend, OR 97701
(541) 318–4733 or (708) 534–9263
idyewool@mindspring.com
bootscoj@attbi.com

Ruckman Mill Farm
Original designs by Susan Feller
Celebration X entry winner.

Patterns drawn on monks cloth or linen.
Send $5 for pattern catalog.
P.O. Box 409, Augusta, WV 26704
www.ruckmanmillfarm.com

Rug Hooking
supplies,
patterns,
equipment,
wool & designs.

(503) 631–2744
17145 S. Seal Ct.
RUG ART & SUPPLY Oregon City, OR
by Suzi 97045-9321

E-mail: suzi@rugartsupply-suzi.com
www.rugartsupply-suzi.com

RUG HOOKING RESOURCES

A Passion for the Creative Life

Textiles to Lift the Spirit by rug hooking artist Mary Sheppard Burton

Sign of the Hook Books

1 (301) 977–1242
www.marysburton.com

SPRUCE RIDGE STUDIOS

Kris Miller
1786 Eager Rd.
Howell, MI 48855

(517) 546–7732
e-mail:
spruceridge@earthlink.net
www.spruceridgestudios.com

Delightful original primitive rug
hooking patterns & supplies

SPRUCE TOP RUG HOOKING STUDIO

255 W. Main Street
Mahone Bay, NS,
Canada B0J 2E0

Rug hooking and braiding courses, retail supplies/ equipment, museum and gallery

1-888-Rug Hook
www.comsearch-can.com/RUGHOOK.htm

Cutting is a *SNAP* With the.....
TOWNSEND FABRIC CUTTER

Quickly snap a cutter cartridge in and go! Cutter Cartridges available in a variety of sizes from a #3 through #10. Also a #8.5!
CALL
TOLL FREE **1-877-868-3544**
www.townsendfabriccutter.com

Turkey Hollow Primitives

Rug Hooking Studio
(203) 263-0426
By Appointment Anytime

Rug Hooking Supplies, Kits, Hand-dyed wool, Individual instruction & monthly workshops. Finished Rugs Available.

www.turkeyhollow primitives.com

Sharon Mathers
Woodbury, CT

WHISPERING HILL FARM

Donna Swanson
Route 169
South Woodstock, CT
06267

(860) 928-0162 • FAX (860) 963-7732
Specializing in rug hooking supplies and out-of-print rug hooking books.

www.webtravels.com/whispering.hill
E-mail: whisperhill@earthlink.com

706 Brownsville Rd.
Sinking Spring, PA
19608
The Wool Studio
Rebecca Erb
tel/fax 610-678-5448
Rug hooking supplies and classes

Send $3.00 for wool samples.

E-mail: rebecca@thewoolstudio.com
www.thewoolstudio.com

Woolley Fox ®

PRIMITIVE RUG PATTERNS
By BARBARA CARROLL

132 Woolley Fox Lane
Ligonier, PA 15658
724 – 238 – 3004
www.woolleyfox.com

EST. 1830
WOOLRICH
The Original Outdoor Clothing Company™

RUG HOOKING FABRIC
Buy Direct from the Factory
Made in the USA • 100% Virgin Wool
Permanently Moth Proofed

Order Toll Free: 1–877–512-7305
Ask for Operator 256

Books From *Rug Hooking*

Books written with the specific needs of rug hookers in mind include **Recipes from the Dye Kitchen,** based on Maryanne Lincoln's magazine column, and **The Complete Natural Dyeing Guide** by Marie Sugar, a volume containing 89 dyeing recipes by an expert natural dyeing instructor. **Hooking With Yarn** by Judy Taylor expands the versatility of hooking through the author's many uses of yarn. Beginners and rug hookers with years of experience will benefit from the wide variety within **Basic Rug Hooking,** from the editors of **Rug Hooking** magazine. Polly Minick's **A Rug Hooking Book of Days** features her primitive rugs and allows a reader to enjoy her work while recording appointments or hooking-related journal entries.

New books to appear by the end of 2003 are **The Secrets of Finishing Hooked Rugs** by Margaret Siano with Susan Huxley and **The Secrets of Primitive Rugs** by Barbara Carroll with Susan Huxley.

Our **web site** (*www.rughookingonline.com*) is packed with vivid photos, informative text, and links to other helpful sites. **Rug Hooking's** objective is to be the primary source of information and inspiration for rug hookers of all levels of experience.

For more information on **Rug Hooking** magazine and its other publications, write to 1300 Market Street, Suite 202, Lemoyne, PA 17043-1420 or call (800) 233-9055. *www.rughookingonline.com*.

ORGANIZE YOUR MOST USEFUL RUG HOOKING RESOURCE

Rug Hooking Binders

Each issue of **Rug Hooking** magazine is packed with invaluable tips, techniques, and resources that will fulfill your hooking needs for years to come. But what happens when you need your January/February 2001 issue, and it's lost under a stack of wool?

Rug Hooking binders eliminate scavenger hunts for back issues of *Rug Hooking* forever! With these handsome burgundy binders, all your back issues will be right at your fingertips. *Rug Hooking*'s classic magazine binders:

- Conveniently hold two full years of *Rug Hooking* magazine.
- Feature an elegant hard-bound finish in luscious burgundy with silver foil lettering.
- Provide twelve removable wires for easy placement and removal of magazines.
- Are a beautiful addition to any bookshelf (or wool shelf, for that matter!)

Plus, our binders also hold all your **Rug Hooking** *books!*

BONUS OFFER
Act now, and we will send you a *Rug Hooking* Magazine Index of your choice (1994-1997, 1997-2000, or 2000-2003) for just $2.00!

A Special Offer for *Rug Hooking* Readers

Our handsome binders retail for $10.95 plus shipping. As *Rug Hooking* readers, however, you know that four years of storage is much better than two. Order now, and we will send you two *Rug Hooking* binders for just $19.95, a savings of almost $2.00! Order additional sets, and store your entire library of *Rug Hooking* magazine!

To order one or more of our **Rug Hooking** binders, either complete, cut out, and mail the reply form provided, or if you prefer, call us toll-free at 1-800-233-9055. BUT ACT QUICKLY. THIS IS A LIMITED TIME OFFER.

Return to: R·U·G **HOOKING**
1300 Market Street, Suite 202
Lemoyne, PA 17043-1420

☐ **Yes,** I want to store all my back issues of *Rug Hooking* magazine for easy future use! Send me an individual *Rug Hooking* binder for just $10.95 plus $3.00 shipping and handling, or **sets of two binders for just $19.95 plus $3.00 shipping and handling!**

_____ # of binders requested **($3.00 shipping and handling per order. PA residents add 6% and Canadians add 7% for sales tax.)**

_____ Add on a **Rug Hooking** Magazine Index of my choice for just $2.00!

Please choose one: ☐ 1994 - 1997 Index ☐ 1997 - 2000 Index ☐ 2000-2003 Index

Name _____

Address _____

City/State/Zip _____

Signature _____ Date _____

☐ Bill me ☐ Check or Money order is enclosed. Charge it to my ☐ MasterCard ☐ Visa

Account Number _____ Expiration Date _____

USE YOUR CREDIT CARD AND ORDER TOLL-FREE 1 (800) 233–9055

Experience the Joy of Rug Hooking

Free Beginner's Kit upon payment! A $29.95 Value

Subscribe to Rug Hooking Magazine and take advantage of this special bonus offer!

- *FREE* preview issue
- *Beginner's kit upon payment*

As you work, you find comfort in the look and feel of the wool...in the fluid movement of your hands...and in the painterly design that slowly begins to emerge beneath your fingertips.

See for yourself why *Rug Hooking* is unlike any craft magazine you've ever encountered. Send or call TOLL FREE for your introductory issue today.

MasterCard and VISA Accepted

Rug Hooking **Magazine**
5 issues plus 1 FREE issue for $27.95

1300 Market St., Suite 202 • Lemoyne, PA 17043-142

1 (800) 233–9055
www.rughookingonline.com